T0180609

Practical Spoken Dialog Systems

Text, Speech and Language Technology

VOLUME 26

The titles published in this series are listed on www.wkap.nl/prod/s/TLTB.

Praktical Spoken Dialog Systems

Edited by

Deborah Dahl
Conversational Technologies, Plymouth Meeting, U.S.A.

KLUWER ACADEMIC PUBLISHERS
DORDRECHT / BOSTON / LONDON

A C.I.P. Catalogue record for this book is available from the Library of Congress.

ISBN 1-4020-2675-7(PB)
ISBN 1-4020-2674-9 (HB)
ISBN 1-4020-2676-5 (e-book)

Published by Kluwer Academic Publishers,
P.O. Box 17, 3300 AA Dordrecht, The Netherlands.

Sold and distributed in North, Central and South America
by Kluwer Academic Publishers,
101 Philip Drive, Norwell, MA 02061, U.S.A.

In all other countries, sold and distributed
by Kluwer Academic Publishers,
P.O. Box 322, 3300 AH Dordrecht, The Netherlands.

Printed on acid-free paper

Printed in the Netherlands

For Rich, Sarah, and Peter

TABLE OF CONTENTS

viii

PREFACE

Deployed spoken dialog systems, in which humans and computers engage in a conversation using speech, are becoming increasingly commonplace. This book includes papers on a variety of topics organized around the theme of what it really takes to build a successful spoken dialog system. Working spoken dialog systems need to take into account both principles of human-computer communication as well as the considerable fund of practical knowledge that is developing in the industry as more and more of these applications are developed and used. The goal of this book is to provide a resource for managers, developers, and students who want to gain insight into both the communication principles of human-computer dialog systems as well as the details of what it takes to design, develop, and deploy a working spoken dialog system. In providing this information, this book fills the gap between introductory material and the research literature on human-computer interaction. It is hoped that the reader will take from this book a deeper and fuller understanding of the practical considerations required to turn basic technologies such as speech recognition, dialog design principles, VoiceXML, and design tools into running systems In addition to understanding techniques for developing running systems based on current technologies, it's also valuable to look beyond current technology and to understand what kinds of new capabilities are coming along in the near future, and this book also contains papers that will spark the readers' imaginations in that direction.

Specific topics covered in the papers in this book include the business aspects of deciding how a speech application will address business needs, several advanced design topics, an in-depth look at how a specific application works in practice, and examples of near-term research work.

Deborah A. Dahl

CONTRIBUTORS

Samuel Bayer, *The Mitre Corporation*

Deborah A. Dahl, *Conversational Technologies*

Morena Danieli, *Loquendo Vocal Technologies*

Kurt Godden, *General Motors R&D*

Li Gong, *SAP Labs*

Robert Keiller, *VoxSurf*

James A. Larson, *Intel Corporation*

Judith A. Markowitz, *J. Markowitz, Consultants*

Clifford Nass, *Stanford University*

Candace L. Sidner, *Mitsubishi Research Laboratories*

Suzanne Liebowitz Taylor, *Unisys Corporation*

INTRODUCTION

The number of deployed spoken dialog systems has exploded in the last few years. In hundreds of applications running all over the world, people can now speak to computers and have them perform useful tasks — make travel reservations, provide news or weather information, read email — based only on the users' speech. These spoken dialog systems combine the technologies of automatic speech recognition, speech synthesis, natural language processing and dialog control to create effective spoken human-computer dialog systems.

The recent explosion of systems is due to a combination of several factors — greatly improved speech recognition technology, the vision and energy of the entrepreneurs who've taken the risk of bringing this speech technology to market, and most recently, the development of standards such as VoiceXML (Voice eXtensible Markup Language) [1] that dramatically lower the barrier to application development.

One of VoiceXML's most appealing features is that it takes very little time to grasp the basic ideas and start generating simple speech applications. There are a number of good ways to get this basic knowledge, including books such as [2, 3] and the VoiceXML specification itself. But these exploratory applications are a long way from deployed, 24/7 systems running in the field.

This book is aimed at addressing the question of what it means to go beyond these first applications, not only for applications built in VoiceXML, but for speech applications in general. Certainly one way of going beyond simple applications is to build more complex applications, with more functionality and more complex back-end integration, such as integration with the web and with back-end databases. There are very good books that can help the developer move forward in this direction, for example, [4, 5]. There are also very good existing books that can help designers create more sophisticated and user-friendly designs by understanding the principles of human factors of spoken dialog such as [3, 6, 7].

This book tackles other dimensions of spoken dialog applications. What this book does is start filling in the gap between the kinds of simple applications that can be built in a few hours, and effective, practical, dialog applications that solve real problems for customers. There are many issues around this topic, and this book is only a start. The papers in this book discuss the issues of the importance of understanding the customer's needs and expectations regarding speech applications (Taylor) advanced design issues (Larson, Nass, Danieli, Godden), incorporation of new technologies like speaker verification (Markowitz), the role of design tools (Dahl), practical issues in deployment of systems using VoiceXML in particular (Keiller) and ideas for future directions in dialog technology (Bayer, Sidner). We focus here on what can be accomplished with both today's technology, and with technology that will be available within the next few years. Because it is focused on current and near-term technology, the book doesn't attempt to cover the rich research literature on spoken dialog systems, although many of the individual papers include pointers into this literature which the interested reader can follow to explore the research issues in more depth.

The book is organized roughly around the application development life cycle, from initial customer discussions through to the details of a fully deployed system, and then concludes with two papers looking to the future. Because VoiceXML is a popular and well-known dialog design framework, many of the papers use VoiceXML to provide very concrete examples of the principles they discuss. However, the principles are applicable to spoken human-computer dialogs in general, regardless of the implementation technology.

Part 1 discusses the initial stages of a project, before design has even begun, with Suzanne Taylor's paper on working with customers in the initial stages of a project. As in any project, technical soundness can't guarantee success if the vendor and customer have different expectations about what the application is and why it's being done. Taylor lays out in detail the numerous considerations of business drivers, environment, customer readiness, and requirements, that have to be gotten right at the outset in order for a project to be successful.

Once the initial selection of the project is completed, design begins. Part 2 covers a wide range of design issues, including the specialized topics of designing speech recognition grammars and speaker authentication systems. Part 2 begins with Clifford Nass and Li Gong's paper on ten important principles based on the evolution of human communication capabilities that have to be taken into account to build effective dialog systems. They make a compelling and insightful claim: Because speech evolved over millions of years for human-to-human communication, it includes many properties that need to be accommodated in understanding human to computer communication.

Most spoken dialog systems have to accommodate both novice and experienced users. A system designed only for novice users will bore experienced users, but novices will be confused by a system designed only for experienced users. James Larson's paper provides guidelines for designing systems for novice, average, and experienced users, as well as techniques for accommodating a spectrum of user capabilities in a single system.

Errors are inevitable in spoken dialog systems. Misrecognitions by automatic speech recognition systems are an obvious source of errors, but as Morena Danieli points out in her paper, many errors originate from systems which can't handle user's natural behavior in error recovery situations. Danieli provides ten best practices for adding effective error recovery capabilities to dialog systems.

When the time comes to put the principles from the papers by Nass and Gong, Larson, and Danieli into practice, developers will look for tools that can assist them in this complex task. My own paper discusses a number of approaches to visualizing spoken dialogs that have been incorporated into existing dialog development tools, or which might be incorporated into future tools. This information will be very useful in the process of selecting design tools.

Designing spoken dialog systems includes designing not only the dialog itself, but also the grammars that support automatic speech recognition. This is a complex task that is extremely important to a successful speech system. Kurt Godden's paper provides eight very useful guidelines for designing good speech grammars.

The last paper in Part 2 is Judith Markowitz's paper on designing for speaker authentication. Many applications need to restrict their access to specific users. Speaker authentication technologies make it possible to base this restriction on the speaker's voice. In addition to providing guidelines for the use of speaker authentication technologies in dialog systems, Markowitz's paper also provides a good introduction to these technologies that will be useful for those who are less familiar with this topic.

Part 3 covers deployment of spoken dialog systems, with Robert Keiller's case study of a specific system implemented by VoxSurf using VoiceXML. He describes the VoxSurf application as well as many important issues that arise in deployment of a full-scale spoken dialog system. These include runtime issues such as speed and latency as well as issues that arise in the use of other technologies, such as output pre-processing for speech synthesis systems. Keiller concludes with some suggestions for improvements to future versions of VoiceXML.

In Part 4 we move beyond today's currently deployed systems and take a look at some future directions in dialog systems. While today's deployed systems typically use either a proprietary architecture or VoiceXML, there are also other innovative open architectures resulting from research efforts. Samuel Bayer's paper discusses the Galaxy Communicator system. The Communicator program provides a framework for integrating research contributions from different sites so that each site can focus on its own area of expertise.

As impressive as today's systems are compared to the systems which were available only a few years ago, there are still significant areas for improvement. Today's systems don't have a high level understanding of the task that the user is attempting to accomplish, so they aren't capable of assisting users in the achievement of their goals. The final paper in the book, Candace Sidner's paper on collaborative interface agents, provides an intriguing picture of sophisticated dialogs with a collaborative agent that can do much of the detailed planning which has to be done by the user in current systems.

I hope you find the papers in this book as useful, thought provoking, and insightful as I do.

Deborah A. Dahl

REFERENCES

[1] W3C, "Voice Extensible Markup Language (VoiceXML 2.0) http://www.w3.org/TR/voicexml20/", http://www.w3.org/TR/voicexml20/, 2002.
[2] M. Miller, VoiceXML: 10 Projects to Voice-Enable Your Web Site. New York: Wiley Publishing, Inc., 2002.
[3] J. A. Larson, VoiceXML: Introduction to developing speech applications. Upper Saddle River New Jersey: Prentice Hall, 2002.
[4] E. A. Andersson, S. Breitenbach, T. Burd, N. Chidambaram, P. Houle, D. Newsome, X. Tang, and X. Zhu, Early Adopter VoiceXML. Birmingham, UK: Wrox Press, 2001.
[5] C. Sharma and J. Kunins, VoiceXML. New York: John Wiley and Sons, Inc., 2002.
[6] B. Balentine and D. Morgan, How to build a speech recognition application. San Ramon, California: Enterprise Integration Group, 1999.
[7] D. Gardner-Bonneau, Human Factors and Voice Interactive Systems. Boston: Kluwer Academic Publishers, 1999.

PART 1

INITIAL STAGES

Chapter 1

Beyond Technology
Preparing for a Successful Speech Engagement

Suzanne Liebowitz Taylor
Unisys Corporation

Key words: speech application development methodology, speech deployment

Abstract: The likelihood of a successful speech application engagement increases significantly if customer business drivers, business practice and environment are considered prior to any application design or implementation. This article discusses our process of discovery with a customer in which we explore all these areas to arrive at a concrete plan for an engagement.

1. INTRODUCTION

There has been a running joke in our organization for the last five years; each year we predict that "next year is the year of Speech". Joking aside, speech technologies have demonstrated extraordinary progress over the last 5 years and the industry is experiencing accelerated growth. As the industry expands business executives are expecting speech-enabled applications to improve their bottom line through cost reductions and new services revenue. In both cases, delivering successful speech-enabled application projects is an imperative for internal IT staff and professional services firms.

This article provides a framework for success in deploying speech solutions, based on our experience (both successes and failures) as consultants in the areas of telephony speech application development and deployment. The term 'consultant' is used to mean someone who has a wide background, depth of experience and skill in the technology and business areas that are required. Consultants wear many hats; therefore, we will also use the terms application developer and system integrator, interchangeably in this discussion.

A speech (or voice) solution is an application or suite of applications where the primary communication mechanism between the user and the computer is through spoken input. Many different technologies, such as speech recognition, text-to-speech synthesis, natural language processing, are employed.

Consider Figure 1 which shows the sequence of interactions between the caller and the voice-enabled application. The end user calls the application via a telephone and is greeted with a pre-recorded or computer synthesized prompt. The end user responds to the prompt. Within the application, the speech recognition engine converts this response to a string of text. Grammars are used by the speech recognizer to anticipate the caller's response, i.e., specify the responses that the recognizer listens for. Natural language processing interprets the meaning of the response and then the application performs an appropriate action based on what the caller requested. The application then responds with another prompt, and the cycle continues until the goal of the caller is accomplished and/or the application or caller hangs up.

The application interface can be thus considered a *conversation* between the caller and the application used to achieve a specific goal. This goal could be, for example, making an airline ticket reservation, checking for the latest sports score, checking for new voice or e-mail messages, or asking the application to call a particular person by name.

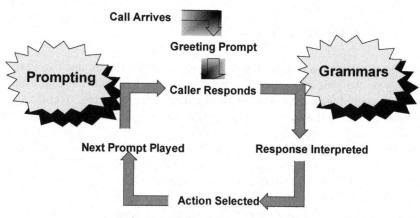

Figure 1. Voice driven application

The effectiveness of this conversation from the caller's point-of-view depends on several factors: how well and clearly the prompt wording is designed, how well the speech recognition engine is able to correctly translate the caller response, whether the result from the speech recognition engine is interpreted correctly and finally, whether the application performs the appropriate action. The prompting of the application then provides output to guide the caller's response and the grammar describes what are acceptable responses to the prompts by the caller.

Although many technologies interplay for the application to work, it takes much more than just good technology to create a successful solution. The solution must satisfy the business goals of the client and the needs of the end users. Success depends on: customer readiness and proper application selection. If these elements are in place and the project is executed properly, the engagement is highly likely to achieve the intended end goal: satisfied customers and satisfied end-users. We ascertain a customer's readiness, prepare for an engagement, and select the solution goals through a process called Discovery. Since Discovery is one step along the way of a speech engagement, we devote some space in Section 2 for a general discussion on what a speech engagement involves and a discussion on the development methodology for a speech engagement.

In Section 3, we dive into the discovery process. We detail how we determine customer readiness by highlighting questions and situations we consider at each stage, and by outlining a series of best practice guidelines. Even with a willing and ready customer, the application must suit the end users needs and make sense from both a business perspective, as well as a technology perspective. Even the best technology will not guarantee user acceptance and usage.

2. SPEECH ENGAGEMENTS

We start with a short digression in this section to describe speech engagements and our speech application development methodology. There will be references to these topics in Section 3

2.1 Types of Speech Engagements

Speech engagements can take several different forms. Some are ends to themselves, and others are building blocks to future engagements. We categorize the types of engagements into the following categories: Discovery, Simulation, Prototype, Pilot, Deployment and Post-Deployment. Together these can also be thought of as phases through the lifecycle of a full-scale speech deployment.

The goal of Discovery is to prepare for the implementation of a speech application, whether it is a prototype or a full deployment. Simulation and Prototype Phases are used to validate designs, build business cases, compare different approaches and methods and/or verify usability with the customer prior to any major implementation efforts. This leads to cost savings for the customer. A Pilot is a small-scale deployment and Post-Deployment covers maintenance and future features of an application.

We briefly summarize each type of engagement, but the discussion in Section 3 will detail the importance and our process through Discovery.

2.1.1 Discovery Phase

The objective of the discovery phase is to achieve customer readiness and the goals of a development engagement. A development engagement could be a simulation (for usability studies), a prototype, or a deployment application. The discovery phase covers the education phase: both of the customer and the consultant/implementer. This is the phase of the speech engagement that we discuss in detail in Section 3. The importance of Discovery is to ensure that the application is in line with current business drivers, future business goals, and technology capability.

2.1.2 Simulation

The application is simulated in order to give the listener a feel for the intended application with employing all the technologies necessary for a full implementation. We use computer simulation tools that enable a caller to call into the simulated application under the same circumstances that he/she would use the final application. Simulation requires human intervention, as a user acts as the speech recognizer and natural language processor. This approach allows us to validate the design prior to any development (and prevent costly errors later in the project), usability testing (to validate user acceptance of the interface concept), or to sell the idea of speech as an interface to stakeholders within the customer's organization or company. The simulation typically has less functionality than the intended end application and targets specific aspects of the user interface.

2.1.3 Prototype Development

The prototype is similar to a simulation in that it usually does not have full functionality of the final application. However, it is a stand-alone application, complete with speech recognition and natural language processing. The application usually runs on a low-line, low-cost platform. Two uses of the prototype are the same as uses for the simulation: usability testing and selling of idea to stakeholders. It also provides validation of the speech recognition technology and, because no human intervention is required, can be used to conduct larger usability trials. The benefits of the prototype are to validate user acceptance prior to any large-scale development of the application and conduct larger user trials. For example, our customers have used the prototype concept to compare different approaches to user interface design, validate user acceptance of the speech interface, and compare user reaction to DTMF versus speech interfaces.

2.1.4 Pilot

A pilot is a limited deployment of the application. It has the full functionality of the deployment system or is part of a gradual rollout of the deployment system. The Pilot is again another step in obtaining user acceptance of the application and is essential for application tuning (e.g. 'tweaking' to get the application right). The most significant use is for recognizer grammar tuning, however, it can also be used for prompt tuning. If the engagement has performed usability studies using simulations and/or prototypes, it is unlikely that any major changes to the system in terms of call flow will be required. The Pilot stage is used to fix any kinks in the system with limited impact to the users and significantly increases the likelihood of successfully deployment.

2.1.5 Deployment

This phase is the full deployment of the application with complete architectural and infrastructure implementation.

2.1.6 Post Deployment Enhancements

During post deployment, periodic tuning of the grammars is performed. This tuning becomes less frequent the longer the application is deployed. This phase allows for new features and enhancements and maintenance of the application which the application in line with business and technology drivers, continued standards compliance and continued end user satisfaction. The goal is to minimize the total cost of ownership of the application.

2.2 Application Development Methodology

The development of the speech application is as much an art as a science, particularly in the area of the user interface design. No matter how wonderful the technology components are, if the user interface is not palatable to the user, the application will not be accepted and is, hence, a failure. The user needs to get to their goal quickly and efficiently.

Therefore, we developed a speech application development methodology (*Figure 2*) which emphasizes user acceptation and quality delivery. Some of these components of this methodology (shown in bold in *Figure 2*) are standard to any software development program (e.g., Project Management, Requirements and Application Definition). The components in bold: Dialog Design, Dialog Validation, Prompt Preparation, Grammar Development, Natural Language Interpretation, and Call Flow Development are specific to speech application development. The sequence of events in this methodology is not linear, but rather groups of iterative activities.

The Dialog Design, Dialog Validation and Prompt Preparation cycle is employed as many times as necessary to come to an agreement on the dialog and prompt design prior to any application coding. A typical implementation of this cycle is the following. The application designer completes an initial design and validates it through simulation. After adjusting the dialog design from the results of the simulation, the prompts are prepared and recorded (if voice talent is to be used). The application developer can also use the simulation tool at this point to validate the design with the customer (with or without recorded prompts). When the application designer and customer accept the dialog design, we are ready to conduct usability tests with typical end users.

Therefore, simulation is used by the developer to validate the intent of the original design, with customer stakeholders to confirm that the design meets expectations, and finally with typical end users to validate usability of the design. In any of these stages, the design can be dialog refined and simulated as many times as necessary.

This methodology also relates the engagement types described in Section 2. On the input side, the information found through the discovery process impacts every stage of the development cycle. We've already discussed the ways in which Simulation is used. Prototypes, pilots and full-scale deployments require all the steps through Deployment, however, the level-of-effort required for each will change with the size of the deployment. Prototypes are typically used for another validation of user acceptance and to refine grammars. Pilots are used to validate the implementation and also to refine grammars (as needed).

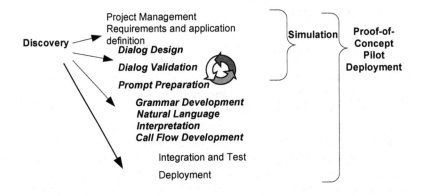

Figure 2. Speech Application Development Methodology

3. DISCOVERY

Discovery is a customer interaction that leads the way to an implementation engagement. The goal of discovery is to achieve customer readiness for entering into an implementation engagement. During this process we collect key information from the customer to bolster the probability of success of the engagement.

We also relate how the selection of the particular application is a critical success factor.

3.1 Customer Role

What role does the customer play during Discovery and the rest of the project? The customer should be a partner in the project. The customer needs to understand the technology, its capabilities and the appropriateness of use. The industry is not at the point yet where speech applications are off-the-shelf and ready-to-go. Even with reusable applications and components, each application needs to be customized, tuned, and tweaked in some way for each customer. These adaptations can include selection of application personality, prompt design, content design, and grammar tunings. To perfect the application, usability tests, pilots and iterative tuning are needed. The customer needs to understand the development process and be willing to be an active part of that process. A ready customer understands its end user population, business goals and success criteria.

3.2   Customer Readiness

3.2.1 Stages

We encounter customers in various states of readiness to accept voice access to information as an integral part of their business environment. Customers may have researched the technology and know that their competition is using it. The customers may be unsure on whether the technology is right for their business. Others know that they want speech, but not how to effectively use it. Some customers come prepared with an exact application in mind, even to the point having a draft of the call flow prepared. Some have prejudices about the technology that need to be dissuaded.

Preparing a customer for an engagement is a two-way conversation. Identifying where the customer is in terms of readiness to accept speech into their business environment helps to identify the type of interactions required for the pre-development phases of the engagement.

Readiness is generally defined in four general stages: Learning/Exploring (Stage I), Want it (Stage II), Ready to Go (Stage III) and Veteran (Stage IV). These stages are not necessarily unique to voice application development, but the processes that we use to work with the customer have components that are specialized to the speech application development process. Stages I – III build upon each other. Stage IV is an extension of Stage III where the customer has previous experience with voice interface applications.

In any case, if a customer comes to us for the first time appearing to be in Stage II – IV, a review of the knowledge that should have been obtained in the previous stages is prudent to ensure that all parties are aligned. It is usually appropriate to backtrack a little and review the information that is available in each stage as appropriate.

3.2.1.1   Readiness Stage I: Learning/Exploring
In Stage I the customer has conducted some research on the market and/or technology. They may think that they might need speech-enablement as a competitive advantage or discriminator, or are being proactively solicited for the engagement. At this point, the customer needs to be educated on the current state-of-the industry, the possibilities and limitations of the technology and what factors will determine a good return on investment for their business.

3.2.1.2   Readiness Stage II: Want it
In this stage, the customer has a good foundation on the base technology and state of the industry. The customer is interested in determining how/if

speech-enablement can be used in their business. If we did not work with the customer through State I, then we review the customers' understanding to ensure that it is consistent with the current state of the art (and not over-hyped or based on out-of-date information). We prefer to engage this stage through interactive workshops designed to hone in on applications that are well suited for the technology as well as satisfy the business criteria for return on investment and success. The desired outcome of this stage is a go forward plan of concrete actions and activities to help the customer achieve the business goals.

The success of this interaction relies on the participation and preparedness of all parties involved. The consultant participating in these sessions is prepared with industry best practices; the customer is expected to provide input on their current business practices, customer offerings and future directions. The go forward plan can lead to any of the engagement phases: usability study with simulation or prototypes, a pilot implementation or a full deployment of one or more voice-access systems. Many times the plan includes all three phases, staged appropriately.

3.2.1.3 Readiness Stage III: Ready to Go

A customer who has completed the first two stages has identified a concrete plan for voice-enablement. At this point, we are ready to move to a more requirements phase.

Sometimes a customer will approach us with a specific application or study already in mind (sometimes to the point of having a call flow design). In this case, we perform a mini Learning/Exploring and Wanting stages to verify that the business and technical requirements are aligned and insure that we understand all these requirements. The application requirements are reviewed in terms of business requirements before moving to the technical phases of the project.

3.2.1.4 Readiness Stage IV: Veteran

Stage IV, which we term the Veteran stage, is really an adjunct to Stage III. The veteran is a customer with previous experience with a speech deployment. However, even if a customer has previous experience, this does not mean that we will not need to work through any of the previous stages for a new engagement.

Understanding the nature of the customer's previous experience with speech-enablement will determine how much educating of the customer we need to do. This experience may have been positive or negative. Some very early trials with speech were so negative that people have been hesitant to deploy the technology. However, whether the past experience was positive or negative, an experienced customer often has some sense of what is involved with both the technology and the process. Since some of these experiences may cause pre-conceived notions that could be barriers to the project ahead, go through a realignment to ensure that the customer's understand of the technology is current (as the technology changes very quickly), and relevant to the project at hand.

3.2.2 Assessing Customer Readiness

There are several areas of information to address when assessing current customer readiness and to reach full readiness. Specifically, what education (or re-education) at each stage will be needed to move forward to the application portion of the project?

3.2.2.1 State of the Industry

The customer should understand the current state of the industry and technology. This includes both the future potential and the current limitations. The objective is to set realistic expectations on what can and cannot be done and what has and has not been done. In this arena, the technology continues to improve and the standards around the speech industry continue to evolve. These changes have implications on the lifetime and maintenance of the application.

We often encounter some confusion on what the particular components of a speech application are. Particularly, we find there is confusion on the terminology of the industry and often need to first explain the differences among *speech recognition* (the conversion of voice waves to text), *natural language* (interpreting the meaning of the speech recognizer output), *text-to-speech technology* (using computer simulated voice to play back prompts or messages to the caller), *recorded voice talent* (used for voice prompts), *dictation* (speaker dependent recognition of voice input, usually used through microphone input), and *speaker verification* (identifying the speaker through a voice print).

The other thing customers need to understand is the current state of voice application standards. At the time of this writing, we see deployments using VoiceXML 2.0 [1] and announcements of new multi-model specifications including Speech Application Language Tags (SALT) [2] and XHTML+Voice [3].

Where just a few years ago, recognizers integrated with proprietary IVR software, the existence of the open standard VoiceXML (and others emerging in the multi-modal space) will eventually make IVR software obsolete.

Is the customer prepared to accept the current standards evolution? What is the price of replacing existing IVR systems? The current specification of

VoiceXML, for example, does not support certain telephony functions that are required by some applications, so proprietary extensions are still used.

3.2.2.2 Involvement in Development Methodology

As a more tactical issue, we ensure that the customer understands the application development process and methodology (as described in Section 2.2) and specifically their role. This is very important as the methodology is an iterative approach and has a significant impact on user acceptance. If the customer accepts a speech project, then to insure its success, they must be willing to participate in focus groups, studies, user trials and pilots in order to perfect the user interface. It is advantageous for the customer to understand the up-front the commitment and partnership that is required for the success of the engagement. Let's look at some components of the human factors considerations. *Figure 3* illustrates some of the information that a customer provides that has profound impact on the user interface – marketing goals, end user targets, personality, etc. If this information is not available or accurate, then user acceptance of the application is in jeopardy.

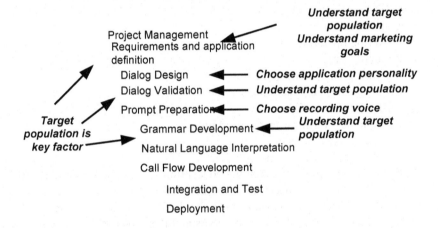

Figure 3. Implications of customer participation on User Interface Design and End user acceptance

3.2.2.3 Previous experience

A customer's previous experience with touchtone and/or voice systems strongly influences their perceptions and attitudes. We support engagements where we perform application development and system integration, as well as provide support for the customer who do their own application development. We have customers that want to keep application development in-house. Therefore, the customer could have experiences in several different facets: as an implementer, as an application provider or as a consumer of speech technology. It is also important to consider experience with DTMF (touchtone) application technology. This is the place to discuss their misgivings about using the technology and the positive and negative aspects of any previous experience.

3.2.2.4 Business Drivers

The customer has a responsibility during the Discovery process as both the provider of information, as well as the consumer. When we have discussions on business drivers for a speech engagement, the onus falls on the customer to provide the pertinent information. The role of the consultant is as a facilitator and consumer of the information. We can provide models and examples from industry, but only the customer knows their business best. The consultant pushes the customer to think about those business drivers that are not fully fleshed out.

The customer should define their success criteria - what would a successful speech application do for their business. The customer should identify the key business drivers for these success criteria. The most common drivers are:

- Lowering operating costs
- Reducing staff
- Increasing customer satisfaction
- Creating revenue-generating services.
- Customer satisfaction
- Creating new business areas/offerings
- Competitive advantages
- Reaching more customers

We have seen projects die in the conception stage because the marketing organizations are not sufficiently involved with the technology organizations in the up-front planning. The customer should understand their go-to-market strategy. The customer should also understand its target end-user population. The nature of the end-user population has implications on the marketing strategy as well as in the design of the application itself. Answers to these questions will effect, for example, whether the application be available in multiple languages. Will the application serve a diverse or homogeneous end user base? Is the user based geographically or globally dispersed?

Although we have not discussed how a particular application is chosen for deployment, it is important to know whether the customer has already identified applications for appropriate use of the technology and provides the appropriate business case (as discussed in the previous section). There are other marketing factors that will influence the application besides the characteristics of the end caller population. For example, the customer may have known brand recognition (in terms of a logo, personality or voice talent (if the customer currently has touch-tone or speech applications). Is it required that new applications use these same brand recognitions?

This brings us back to the discussion around *Figure 3* in Section 3.2.2.2. During requirements and application definition, it is critical to continue to align with the target end user population and the marketing goals of the organization. During dialog design, these factors are used to choose the application personality and during prompt design, the application voice.

3.2.2.5 Understanding the customer's environment

It is equally important to understand the customer's present and, if planned, future environment. By environment, we mean both the technical infrastructure as well as traffic and use projects. Understanding the customer environment is an iterative process. First we get a general understanding of the topics discussed in this section. Once the application project is determined, probe into the environmental details that will specifically impact the project (e.g., databases, data feeds, telephony lines, etc.). Some of these topics will be revisited several times with the customer. We will touch on some of the areas that we typically investigate during the Discovery process.

Usage projections. Is information available in order to project the application usage? We ask about both agent and touchtone systems are about annual call volume, percentage of return calls to the system, and average call time. If the application is a replacement or enhancement to legacy touchtone systems, we try to understand the percentage of calls handled by the current IVR and the average handling time of the system.

What are the current phone charges per minute and are there domestic and international calls? How many in-coming telephone lines and the type? In a call center, how many agents are there?

Integration Requirements. Most applications do not operate in a vacuum. To access technical feasibility, all integration requirements must be understood. Look at any legacy system interface requirements, and if the legacy systems are not easily compatible with the planned architecture, explore what alternatives are available. What are the data feeds for the application? Will the application interface with databases, the World Wide Web, or other applications that scrape information from other Internet sites or a combination?

What about Network/Host connectivity and Telephony requirements? What is the Computer Telephone Integration Requirement? Are other services (e.g., FAX back) required?

Information Access and Presentation. The world is heading towards multi-modal access and multimodal presentation of the data. In this particular application how will the data be presented to the end user? How do current and future customers access information? Will there be multiple access modes (e.g., phone, web browser, WAP, etc.) to the same data?

We need to consider where the information has to come from. It may come from existing or to-be developed databases or from third party information providers. It will be possible in the future for an end-user to be able to phone an application and observe interactions via the Internet browser or a hand-held. Most customers are not at this level of sophistication today, but it is not that far in the future to start planning or consider the implications on applications in the future.

3.3   Identifying Candidate Applications

Finally we align the technical feasibility of an application with the business drivers, business practices, customer environment, and go to market strategy. Cost is always a factor, but first identifying candidate applications based on technical and business drivers is prudent. Later it will be necessary to calculate the return on investment (ROI) on candidate applications to further determine a proper course of action. Most of the speech vendors have templates for calculating return on investment.

Ideas for voice-enabled applications sprout from different seeds. A customer may be looking to replace existing touchtone applications, replace live agent functions, create a speech version of an existing web application or create a new application.

3.3.1 What makes a good application in general?

From a purely technical point of view, we look for applications in which the speech recognition will have the highest success and the dialog will streamline the task for the user. Applications should be measured by task completion, not recognition accuracy. So, in general, the responses are not too open-ended, grammars are not inordinately complex, and information can be acquired in small chunks (either as a dialog technique or as a fall-back technique in natural language or mixed initiative dialog). These statements are a bit of a generality, as with the reality of natural language and mixed initiative more creative dialogs can be used. Also, natural language and recognizer capability are improving the size and complexity of grammars that can be handled and increases in processing power of computer also improve the handling of larger grammars.

Besides the purely technical aspects, we also look at the typical end user. The likelihood of success is higher when users are calm and not irritated when they call. Therefore an order-entry application is a more appealing application to approach than a complaint department application. In the later case, speaking to a human still goes a long way to placating a caller.

3.3.2 Call Center Adopting an Existing Application/ Replacing live function

If the customer has a call center, then applications can replace existing touchtone applications, replace common live agent functions or enhance live agent functions during peak periods. The goals are to reduce call times and, increase agent productivity.

If the goal is to enhance agent functionality, we spend a day or so in the call center listening. What are common, predictable or repetitive tasks? Do these tasks lend themselves to speech? What are the end user population demographics? What is the nature and demeanour of the end users? Instead of replacing all of the live agent function, can part of the function be replaced by speech? The information can be screen-popped to the agent for the remainder of the transaction or interaction.

If the goal is to replace an existing touchtone application then we spend effort listening to the application, understanding its purpose and functionality. We discover from the customer what are the most commonly used functions are and what the least used functions. What are typical completion rates? Any research that is available on the usability of the application is invaluable. We obtain any documented call flows and prompts corresponding to the application. The big payoff for replacing touchtone applications is by shortening the caller experience and/or adding additional functionality that the touchtone system was unable to accommodate. We look for obvious ways to reduce the caller time by flattening touchtone tree menus, providing shortcuts to popular functions, etc.

3.3.3 Web: Speech-enablement of existing Application

In this case the goal is not to replace an existing DTMF application, but to create a voice-enabled version of another type of existing application (typically a web application). We need to understand all the functionality of the existing application and what is easy or more difficult to replicate with voice. The "look and feel" of the existing application can influence the "listen and feel" of the speech application. We will use the application as a typical end user would (not just through demonstrations by the customer). If possible, we get an account on the system and spend some time making realistic transactions.

3.3.4 New application

Sometimes the application idea is brand new and stems from improving a particular business function or creating a new business function. In this case it is important that we understand the customers current or future business practices. We look for practices that can be automated. Consider whether the automation should be just voice or combined with Internet access (and in the near future other modes of interaction).

4. SUMMARY

This article has discussed the importance of the convergence of business drivers, business practice, and technical feasibility in formulating a speech engagement with a customer. The process by which we achieve this is called Discovery. During Discovery we explore in partnership with the customer, all the facets needed to arrive at a concrete plan for an engagement.

By approaching all these areas, the likelihood of a successful engagement is significantly increased. Furthermore, as the state of the technology, as well as the state of the industry are changing rapidly, incorporating both customer future plans and anticipated industry trends into the planning of your project will enhance its appeal. A successful engagement is not just delivering on time and on-schedule, but making sure that the customers and their customers are satisfied with the end product.

REFERENCES

[1] S. McGlashan, D. C. Burnett, J. Carter, P. Danielsen, J. Ferrans, A. Hunt, B. Lucas, B. Porter, K. Rehor, and S. Tryphonas, "Voice Extensible Markup Language (VoiceXML 2.0)", W3C Proposed Recommendation, http://www.w3.org/TR/voicexml20/, 2002.
[2] "Salt Forum", http://www.saltforum.org, 2002.
[3] IBM, "XHTML+Voice", http://www.w3.org/Submission/2001/13/, 2001.

PART 2

DESIGN

Chapter 2

Ten Principles for Designing Human-Computer Dialog Systems
A Perspective from Evolutionary Psychology

Clifford Nass and Li Gong
Stanford University: SAP Labs

Key words: evolutionary psychology, design of spoken dialog systems

Abstract: Speech is not just another technology. Speech as a primary means of communication played a critical role in human evolution. Speech was a unique human faculty and marker until speech technologies were created. However, the slowly-evolving human brain still operates in the same mechanisms when we interact with speech interfaces as when we converse with other people. We identified ten fundamental principles with respect to processing speech, producing speech, and spoken dialogs for humans from the perspective of evolutionary psychology and demonstrated that these principles apply to human users' interaction with speech interfaces. Implications for designing spoken dialog systems are suggested.

1.   INTRODUCTION

Before today's computer systems could produce and recognize speech, speech was a unique faculty and marker of humans. Through the long history of evolution, humans developed exquisite apparatuses and brain functions for producing and processing speech. The human articulator system consists of well-controlled and –coordinated components of tongue, lips, cheeks, and teeth. More of the motor cortex (particularly Broca's area) is devoted to vocalization than any other function, in sharp contrast to every other animal, including primates [1]. Only *Homo sapiens* can produce 14 phonemes per second: Even the Neanderthals could not sustain speech because of the structure of their breathing apparatus [2].

Human ears and brain are also well-designed and evolved for speech recognition and comprehension. Infants as young as one day old show relatively greater left-hemisphere electrical activity to speech sounds, and relatively greater right-hemisphere activity to non-speech sounds [1]. Four days after birth, babies can distinguish the sounds of their native language from sounds of other languages. By adulthood, humans can perceive speech at the phenomenally fast rate of up to 40-50 phonemes per second. Speech is so much a part of being human that people with IQ scores as low as 50 or brains as small as 400 grams can fully comprehend and speak at a competent level [1].

Why did humans develop such advanced and powerful speech faculties? The answer lies in the crucial role played by speech in human evolution. Speech is an essential means of communication between humans. It was through alliance and cooperation with other humans that our ancestors fought animals, harvested foods, and reared children. Without speech and language to accurately convey meanings and intentions in complex situations, humans may not have survived. A rich range of evidence in anthropology, linguistics, and other disciplines has shown that speech and language are a universal faculty and a "human instinct" across cultures [3]. Speech is an essential propellant and intrinsic ability for the survival and growth of individuals, families, and all human groups.

Because speech was a unique and critical human ability, humans evolved so that when they heard a sound, they would very rapidly determine whether it was a speech sound or not. The long history of human evolution has hard-wired our brain to *automatically* equate speech with being human. If speech had been shared by other species, our ancestors would have been easily misled to approach or trust other animals producing speech sound and endanger themselves. This ability meant that humans could rapidly determine whether there was another member of their species in the area, a clear advantage.

However, the equation "*speech = human*" has been challenged recently by the development of speech technology. Speech output and input in various computing devices are becoming more commonplace, including talking toys, telephony-based stock and airline reservation systems, voice-controlled cell phones and PDA's, automobile PCs, computer-synthesized talking heads, and speech recognition word processors, among others. The list of voice-enabled devices and interfaces is growing rapidly because speech provides a natural and easy way to interact with technologies. In some cases, speech represents the only alternative to textual presentation of information for people such as the blind, young children, and illiterates, for eyes-busy environments, and for technologies that cannot present text (e.g., small display areas). How, then, do humans respond to this new "species" of technological artefacts which possess the human capabilities of speaking, listening, or both? Can humans distinguish these machines from people?

For better or worse, new technologies engage old brains. The human brain, shaped through hundreds of thousands of years evolution, responds to speaking/listening technologies as if they were people. Although a user may identify a recorded human voice in a computer with the human whose voice was recorded, this logic cannot apply to clearly computer-synthesized TTS (text-to-speech). A user would also have a hard time associating a "listening" computer, wall-display, or embedded system with any human. Research shows that users do not operate on a mental model imagining the programmer who developed the application when they interact with computers [4]. The direct association between speech and being human is innate, automatic, and unconscious, because throughout human evolution, if one hesitated in judging "Is it human or not" after hearing a speech sound, he or she ran the risk of a slow response in a critical situation.

Humans use the same parts of the brain to listen to computer speech and speak to computers as they listen and speak to other humans. This commonality in the "hardware" and mechanisms in the brain underlies the users' social responses to speech technologies. Recent research has provided clear empirical evidence that users exhibit the same social and human-directed responses to speech interfaces.

This chapter draws out a set of evolutionary principles governing human's processing and production of speech and human-human dialogs and applies these principles to the design of human-computer spoken dialog systems. Relevant research is reviewed to support the principle and its applicability to dialog systems. Implications and open questions for designing speech output and input and human-computer dialogs are proposed.

2. PROCESSING SPEECH

An essential mechanism that humans use to process stimuli, including speech, is categorization. Categorization efficiently helps humans quickly extract essential information from stimuli and preserves their limited cognitive capacity [5]. Basic categories that humans immediately use to process speech include gender, emotion, and personality.

2.1   Principle 1: Gender perception is foremost and powerful

The most important and immediate dimension of categorization of speech is the gender of the speaker. The evolutionary imperative to rapidly identify the sex of another person is obvious: Procreation is the only way for a species to evolve. Gender is so important that instead of being encoded in terms of canonical representation of voices, the distinction of male and female in speech is accomplished via unusually elaborate and complex auditory psychophysical processes involving F0, formant frequencies, breathiness, etc. [6].

Of course, gender is irrelevant to computers; indeed, it would be hard to imagine anything more sexless than a computer screen. However, a study challenged this idea and showed that gender perception and stereotyping due to voices in computers was so powerful that it affected the users' perception of the computers [7]. During the experiment, participants were tutored by a (prerecorded male or female) voice-based computer on a stereotypically "male" topic (computers and technology) and a stereotypically female topic ("love and relationships"). The evaluator computer, using a different prerecorded female or male voice, positively evaluated the performance of the tutor. Consistent with the literature on gender-stereotyping, individuals exhibited the following stereotypes toward the computers: 1) The male-voiced computer received more credit for praise than did the female-voiced computer; 2) praise from the male-voiced computer was more convincing than the female-voiced computer; and 3) the female-voiced tutor computer was rated as significantly more informative about love and relationships and significantly less informative about computers and technology than the male-voiced tutor computer. In post-experiment debriefing, all participants uniformly indicated that male-voiced computers were not different from female-voiced computers and that to engage in gender-stereotyping with respect to computers would be ludicrous.

Gender perception and the effect of voice is so innate and powerful that it applies to computer-synthesized speech, i.e., text-to-speech (TTS). Participants in a study worked with a computer that employed either a synthesized female voice (e.g., F0 = 220 Hz) or a synthesized male voice (F0 =115 Hz) [8]. The participant was confronted with a series of choice dilemmas; for each, the computer would argue for one option over the other. Following gender stereotypes, participants were significantly more likely to accept the male-TTS computer's suggestions than those of the female-TTS one. Remarkably, there were also social identification effects: There was a significant cross-over interaction with respect to trustworthiness and attractiveness, such that people preferred their own (clearly non-human) "gender" for the TTS voice.

Although it may seem surprising that gender effects apply to clearly non-human TTS, the fundamental structures for processing vocal content are very liberal in their categorizations of speech sounds. For example, "dichotic listening tasks" (simultaneously playing different information to each ear) have demonstrated that the right ear (and hence the left hemisphere) has an advantage in processing not only one's native language, but nonsense syllables, speech in foreign languages, and even speech played backwards! Parameters used by human's speech-processing apparatus for distinguishing gender, e.g., fundamental frequency, formant frequencies, and breathiness are applicable to both synthetic voices and human voices.

– *Design Implication*: The gender choice of a TTS voice as well as a recorded human voice is highly consequential. The "casting" of a voice is as important for speech interfaces as it is for traditional media.
– *Design Implication:* Gender effects and stereotypes should be taken into account, although not necessarily conformed to, when designing interfaces.
– *Open Question:* What other demographic characteristics will be recognized by users, and what stereotypes will be elicited by those demographic characteristics?

2.1   Principle 2: Emotion is an essential component of voice

Emotion plays a significant role in human evolution [9]. Emotion prioritizes one's attention and cognitive effort to what is critical for survival [10, 11]. Without the guidance of emotion, a human would find him/herself facing an almost infinite number of stimuli that we could possibly attend to in their surroundings.

Voice is one of the channels carrying emotional cues. The human voice evolved to express emotions in a well-coordinated set of vocal parameters such as pitch, pitch range, volume, and speech rate [12]. Emotion in speech facilitated processing of verbal content, an evolutionary advantage as a listener could discern strong anger in the cry of "attack" and distinguish it from the enthusiastic shout of "a duck" (a food source). The paralinguistic manifestation of emotion was particularly valuable when the semantic content was difficult to discern, for example, when the environment was noisy or when there was language barrier. When one sensed fear in a voice, the listener did not have to comprehend the word "run" to trigger the fleeing mechanism. Thus, attention to and processing of emotional cues provided evolutionary advantages that made emotion detection become a hard-wired and automatic ability.

While the human brain evolved to detect emotion in human speech, research has demonstrated that the same heuristics are applicable to synthetic speech, whether concatenated or acoustically modeled. Concatenated speech realizes emotion by having the reader dictate text with a particular emotional tone, chopping the words into phonemes, and re-assembling the speech segments, retaining the original emotional tone. Systems based on acoustic modeling can directly manipulate the same parameters that are relevant in expression of emotions in human speech. By varying parameters including pitch, timing, voice quality, and articulation, for example, [13] found that users could discriminate anger, disgust, fear, joy, sadness and surprise in TTS.

Identification of emotion in synthetic speech is important, but from the point of view of design, the crucial question is whether the emotions manifested in TTS have the same effect as those in natural human speech. Gong [14] compared a computer-synthesized a talking head with a happy facial expression and happy vocal expression to the same talking head with sad facial and vocal expressions. Both talking heads maintained the same emotion non-adaptively throughout presenting three happy and three sad fictional books. However, the users reported higher likelihood of buying, reading, and recommending the books and more positive attitudinal responses in the happy-talking head condition than in the sad one, i.e., a positivity bias effect. Although TTS was not decoupled from the synthetic face in the study, it suggests that emotions manifested in TTS affect users in the same way as emotions in human speech.

A general propensity that humans inherit and socially develop is to manifest emotions appropriate to the context [15]. A study tested this contextual appropriateness rule with both human speech and TTS [16]. Users listened to a human voice or TTS presenting news stories, movie reviews, and health information with happy and sad content on a telephony application. The emotion manifested in the voice was either consistent or inconsistent with the emotion of the content. People liked the content more when the emotion of the voice matched the emotional tone of the content.

– *Design Implication:* Emotion is an indispensable factor in casting either human or TTS voices. Rather than running the risk of unintentionally conveying undesirable emotion, one should try to tune the voice in a system to express the appropriate emotions.

– *Design Implication*: The contextual appropriateness rule stipulates that the voice in a system should express emotions suitable to the emotional tones of the context. When the voice cannot adapt its emotions to the context, positive emotions are preferred over negative ones.

- *Open Question:* How do users with different personalities and from different cultures differ in their expectation and preference of emotional expressions in a voice?

2.2   Principle 3: Voice manifests personality

After humans extract the gender and emotional information from another person's voice, they turn to a higher-order construct: personality. Personalities are an efficient mechanism to categorize and differentiate countless individuals and help humans interpret and predict others' attitude and behaviors [5, 17]. Without the guidance of personality categorization, humans would find themselves short of time in understanding and predicting the behavior of other people. Despite the risk of overlooking the unique aspects of each individual, personality has the evolutionary value of enabling humans to quickly and efficiently know how to behave toward other individuals and how the other individuals will behave toward them.

Research shows voice carries rich cues about personalities. For example, at least five speech parameters are used to detect extroversion or introversion in another person's voice: speech rate, fundamental frequency, amplitude, pitch range, and amplitude range. Extroverts speak more rapidly and with a higher pitch, louder volume, and greater variance in pitch and volume. A study shows the same parameters manifest personality in TTS [16]. On a simulated book-selling web site, these parameters were manipulated in a TTS voice which presented book descriptions and asked participants about their opinions of the books. The "introverted" or "extroverted" TTS voice presented the descriptions to either extroverted or introverted users. Users accurately recognized the personality cues in TTS. And consistent with the well-documented finding that individuals are attracted to others who are similar to themselves, users who heard a voice that matched their personality were more likely to buy the book and trusted the book descriptions and the reviewer more. They also liked listening to the voice and the reviews more than did those who heard a voice with a dissimilar personality.

Interestingly, the match between the person's *voice* and the TTS voice was irrelevant; it was the participants' actual personality that was definitive. Thus, similarity lies in the cognitive construct of personality rather than in a simple decomposition and matching of features of the voice.

- *Design Implication:* Personality is an important decision in casting a TTS voice as well as a human voice.
- *Open Question:* Should a voice with a particular personality (or gender) be assigned to the user, or should the user be able to select the voice from an array of options?

On the one hand, there is a general design philosophy that "choice is good," and cognitive dissonance theory suggests that people will tend to like the voices they choose (although there is also some evidence for "buyer's remorse"). On the other hand, there is no empirical evidence that individuals will select voices that match their personality, that fit gender stereotypes, or that express the appropriate emotional tone, all of which would tend to increase satisfaction.

2.3 Principle 4: A voice is associated with a face

Every human being has a unique face and a unique voice. Throughout virtually all of human evolution, voice communication was intrinsically face-to-face. Because the face contains so many parts of the vocal apparatus—lips, cheeks, jaw, teeth and tongue—humans intensely watch a person's face to increase comprehension [2].

With 20th-century technologies, it became possible to establish interactive, two-way communication without being physically proximate. The combination of identifiability and the intimate linkage between faces and voices lead individuals to automatically imagine a face when hearing a voice. Although this cognitive creation is not always accurate, it is grounded in the assumption that voices and faces are inextricably linked.

Although the pairing of human faces and voices is genetically determined, this is not the case for synthetic visual speech, i.e., computer-synthesized talking heads. One can choose from a large array of synthetic faces, TTS voices, and recorded human faces and voices.

Although one may be tempted to pair a face and a voice for an interface based on the rule of optimizing the qualities of both face and voice, two studies have shown that consistency between the face and the voice is crucial. In the first study, a synthetic face (Baldi; [2]) was paired with either a TTS voice or a recorded human voice [18]. The talking head asked users a series of open-ended personal questions, e.g., "what do you dislike about your physical appearance?" To control for the main effect of the voice, the researchers examined responses to the voices when a face was not present. Users disclosed more information and the disclosure was more intimate when the synthetic face spoke with TTS than with the recorded human voice. The opposite difference was found for the TTS and human voice alone. This finding suggests that people desire a "consistent" pairing of a synthetic face with a synthetic voice. A follow-up study replicated the same effects and additionally demonstrated a human face speaking with his own voice was more desirable than the same face speaking with synthetic speech [18]. That is, the mismatch between human and synthetic faces and voices seems to violate people's expectation of the "right" face being coupled with the "right" voice. Therefore, the evolved tendency to integrating a face and a voice applies to interfaces as well.

- *Design Implication:* A face is a tremendous enhancement to speech processing if the speech interface has a visual display.
- *Design Implication:* Consistency is an important rule guiding the pairing of a face and a voice. Synthetic faces or voices should not be paired with human voices or faces.

Some existing visual speech interfaces either couple the face of a real human (using thousands of videotaped talking facial images) with TTS or couple a synthetic face with recorded human speech files. Although the natural human face or speech is superior to its synthetic counterpart, the mismatching between them actually reduces the overall quality and appeal of the interface.

3. PRODUCING SPEECH

3.1 Principle 5: Humans speak to express affect as well as meaning

Most existing speech input systems only capture and recognize the verbal content of user's spoken input; the paralinguistic or vocal aspects of user's speech are frequently overlooked. These vocal cues not only provide rich information to aid recognition of user's emotional states but also can help interpret the meaning of the user's input. For example, sarcasm is almost impossible to discern without some attention to the tone of voice. A simple example is the sentence of "I want to receive junk mails" ended with a rising tone will be misinterpreted if the speech recognizer does not capture the tonal feature.

Detection of vocal cues in the user's speech helps recognize the user's physiological and emotional states. Research shows speech is a strong indicator of one's activity or energy level [16]. The same mechanisms identified for generating emotion in speech can be used to detect the emotions of the users. Knowing the user's physiological and emotional states is an essential requirement for making a system intelligent and adaptive. As speech recognizers become more widespread, the ability to extract vocal cues will become ever more important.

- *Design Implication*: Speech systems should incorporate speech feature analysis to capture the physiological and emotional cues in users' spoken input.

- *Design Implication*: Speech systems should mirror the physiological and emotional cues in user's spoken input. For example, the system should mirror the user's tiredness with a slower voice speed and lower pitch.
- *Open question*: How rapidly and obviously should a speech system adapt to the user? Most human adaptations, including speech adaptations, are very subtle. As a result, they tend to affect listeners unconsciously. Will technology-based voices be able to manifest the same subtlety, or will the cues have to be more pronounced?

3.2   Principle 6: Humans speak to be understood

A primary goal of speaking is to be understood by the listener. Although humans have evolved to comprehend speech, we all have experienced interactions in which the other person had difficulty understanding what we were trying to say. These "at-risk" listeners may not be proficient in the particular language we are using, may have difficulty with hearing, or may be distracted, among other inhibitors. Given the desire to be understood and the exquisite control humans have over their speech output, humans use "hyper-articulate" speech (e.g., increased pauses, elongated words) when encountering people who have comprehension difficulties.

Oviatt and colleagues [19] demonstrated that computers that have poor recognition elicit the same adaptive behaviors. They presented users with a system that varied in its recognition failure rate. When the system failed to recognize an utterance, users were instructed to repeat the utterance until they were understood. Consistent with an evolutionary perspective, users exhibited the same adaptations that humans use with non-comprehending human listeners. Specifically, when the system failed, users not only changed the duration and amplitude of speech; during high error rates, they also exhibited fewer disfluencies and more hyper-clear phonological features.

- *Design implication:* Speech recognition systems that learn may not steadily improve, no matter how effective the adaptive algorithms are. Imagine a system that starts out with a high error rate. The user will produce hyper-articulate speech, which the system will then begin to adapt to, reducing its error rate. The user, recognizing that the system is improving its recognition rate, will then adopt less hyper-articulate speech. This will temporarily increase the error rate (because the user will be changing his/her speech pattern) and lead the system to adapt to the new speech pattern. Although the system and the user will eventually stabilize, there will inevitably be fits and starts.

- *Open question:* Will other markers of at-risk listeners, such as the accent of the voice in a spoken dialog system, lead individuals to hyper-articulate in systematic ways?

3.3 Principle 7: Humans speak multimodally

When humans speak, they often move their hands (gestures) to point or provide emphasis [20], present facial expressions to indicate the valence and arousal of the response [11], look at referred objects [21], and move other parts of their bodies to manifest a variety of attitudes and information [22]. Speaking became automatically multimodal for a number of reasons. First, without writing or media for communication, face-to-face communication was the only means for two individuals to transmit information and remains the canonical form of communication [21]. Second, the use of multiple modes made the attempt to communicate much more efficient by reducing ambiguity, as when one points at an object rather than describes it [22]. The ability to quickly notify other members of one's community when danger was near or opportunities were present dramatically increased survival [23].

Another advantage of multimodal interfaces is that they provide cognitive and performance advantages because different modalities tap into different cognitive resources (multiple resource theory) [24, 25]. Research shows that interfaces with multimodal speech input are conducive to spatial-manipulation tasks such as maps and drawing [26] and to hands-busy or eyes-busy situations such as sorting flight baggage [27], and facilitate multi-tasking [28, 29]. Better memory for the information and higher performance in applying the information are found when the data are split in visual and auditory presentation modes [2, 30]. Multimodal presentation of information exploits multiple sensory and processing channels rather than overloads one channel [30].

As a result of these evolutionary advantages, humans do not extinguish their multimodal behaviors and perceptions even when they would be redundant. For example, even when only a single modality can be obtained by a receiver, such as when individuals speak on the phone, people automatically manifest gestures and facial expressions which cannot be seen by the party on other end of the line. Similarly, humans will intensely watch the faces of their interaction partner even when the content is clear and unambiguous.

- *Design Implication:* Speech interfaces are not by definition unimodal in terms of either input or output. Complementary modalities can greatly enhance usability, performance, and appeal.
- *Design Implication:* Inconsistencies across modalities will be highly problematic for users.

- *Open question:* What other modalities in addition to visual (for output) and gesture (for input) are complementary to speech?

Haptics has been used in limited situations [31], but is rarely combined with speech. Taste and smell are yet to be explored as viable modalities for human-computer interaction.

4.   SPOKEN DIALOG INTERACTION

4.1   Principle 8: Social presence is psychologically important

Throughout evolutionary history, the use of speech required the two individuals to be physically close. Physical proximity is important because when another person, especially a stranger, is close, he or she presents the most potential for opportunity or harm; hence, one is cautious in one's interactions. In general, presence, whether real or perceived, of other humans has important psychological consequences [32-37].

To determine whether speaking to a computer would elicit feelings of proximity and thereby would elicit caution, a study by Nass and Gorin [38] had people provide responses to a series of questions for which the socially desirable answer and the truthful answer conflicted (e.g., "I never lie."). Consistent with the idea that speech suggests social presence, participants provided significantly more socially appropriate and cautious responses to the computer when the input modality was voice as compared to mouse, keyboard, or handwriting (the latter allowed us to rule out the novelty of the technology as an alternative explanation for these results).

- *Design Implication:* Criticism from the computer will be much more disturbing in speech systems as compared to systems without the speech component.
- *Design Implication:* Errors and unintelligent behaviors of the computer will be much more consequential in speech systems as compared to systems without the speech component. Negative comments and behaviors are processed more deeply and lead to greater arousal than positive comments [39]. When combined with social presence, these negative behaviors will seem yet more threatening and consequential.

4.1   Principle 9: Humans expect reciprocity and symmetry when they converse

Reciprocity is a general rule governing human-human interaction [40]. When a person speaks to another person, he/she expects the other person to speak back unless that person is prevented doing so by an uncontrollable factor such as aphasia. Otherwise, if the other person violates the rule of reciprocity, for example, gesturing back when spoken to, he/she would trigger distrust and scrutiny. Trust was a crucial factor in humans' collaboration for fighting again enemies, hunting, harvesting, and tending families.

Humans' cognitive and attitudinal mechanisms evolved to prefer symmetry in the modality of interaction. Research on stimulus-response compatibility shows the inherent advantage of matching input and output modalities in human processing and behavior [41]. When stimulus-response modalities are matched, for example, auditory-auditory or visual-visual, studies show that the retrieval of information from memory is faster and task performance is better [42, 43]. In a study with simulated threat-evaluation task, pilots had better performance when the stimulus modality matched the modality in which the pilot made response [41].

- *Design Implication:* A speech interface should allow both speech input and speech output. Exceptions can be made due to users' characteristics (e.g., the deaf or people with aphasia) or due to situational constraints (e.g., the environment is too noisy).
- *Open question:* Should multimodal output match with multimodal input?

4.2 Principle 10: Spoken dialog is a collaborative act

Collaboration is a requirement for sustaining a functional spoken dialog between humans [44]. Clark [21] describes conversation as a waltz, for which seamless coordination between the two dancers is indispensable. Interactants build and maintain common ground supporting their conversation by agreeing on shared topics and reference objects and interpreting each other's meaning and making responses. Spoken dialog without coordination will immediately become dysfunctional and soon break down.

When humans interact with spoken dialog systems, collaboration is once again the cornerstone. Frequently, systems misrecognize users' utterance or give inappropriate responses. Such "misbehaviors" are highly consequential because they break the common ground [44] necessary for dialogs. Commonly used error prompts such as "System error 34159 is encountered" make the problem worse because they clearly indicate that the system is not collaborative. Although great technological improvement in natural language processing, machine learning and adaptation, and artificial intelligence in general is needed to enable computers fully collaborative dialog partners, simple techniques can be readily used to improve a system's collaborativeness.

- *Design implication*: Framing and wording of errors on speech interfaces are crucial. The general guideline is to politely make suggestions. Compared to nonsensible error prompts, sincere apologies in comprehensible words would indicate that the system is trying to communicate and repair the dialog. Making sensible suggestions without blaming or commanding the user implies that the system has the collaborative attitude.
- *Open question:* Would indicators of adaptive and collaborative behaviors of a speech system inflate the users' expectation and, thus, inadvertently hurt the system?

5.   FINAL THOUGHTS

Evolutionary psychology is rarely considered in studying or designing spoken dialog systems or human-computer interaction. Traditionally, understanding of human brain and speech is used to guide the analysis and modeling of cognitive parameters, such as recognition rates, extent of in-grammar utterances, prosody vs. clarity, etc. This chapter provides an initial theoretical framework and empirical evidence that evolutionary psychology can provide important insights into the design of spoken dialog systems. Of course, there is much more known about speech and the human brain than what is presented here, and there are undoubtedly numerous consequences that were not mentioned. Although 21st-century technologies change remarkably fast, creating radical new problems and opportunities for designers, evolution works very slowly and universally. By understanding the old brains that guide every user, designers can be prepared for any technological innovations in spoken dialog systems.

REFERENCES

[1] D. I. Slobin, *Psycholinguistics*, 2nd ed. ed. Glenview, IL: Scott, Foresman and Co., 1979.
[2] D. M. Massaro, *Perceiving talking faces: From speech perception to a behavioral principle*. Cambridge, MA: MIT Press, 1998.
[3] S. Pinker, *The language instinct*. New York, NY: W. Morrow and Company, 1994.
[4] S. S. Sundar and C. Nass, "Source orientation in human-computer interaction: Programmer, networker, or independent social actor?," *Communication Research*, vol. 27, pp. 683-703, 2000.
[5] S. T. Fiske and S. E. Taylor, *Social cognition*. New York, NY: McGraw-Hill, Inc, 1991.
[6] J. W. Mullenix, K. A. Johnson, M. Topcu-Durgun, and L. W. Farnsworth, "The perceptual representation of voice gender," *Journal of the Acoustical Society of America*, vol. 98, pp. 3080-3095, 1995.

[7] B. J. Fogg and C. Nass, "Do users reciprocate to computers?," presented at ACM CHI, 1997.

[8] E.-J. Lee, C. Nass, and S. Brave, "Can computer-generated speech have gender? An experimental test of gender stereotypes.," presented at CHI 2000, The Hague, The Netherlands, 2000.

[9] C. Darwin, *The Expression of the Emotions in Man and Animals*. London: HarperCollins, 1872/1998.

[10] J. Tooby and L. Cosmides, "The past explains the present: Emotional adaptations and the structure of ancestral environments," *Ethology and Sociobiology*, vol. 11, pp. 407-424, 1990.

[11] S. Brave and C. Nass, "Emotion in human-computer interaction," in *Handbook of human-computer interaction*, J. A. Jacko and A. Sears, Eds. New York: LEA Press, in press.

[12] K. R. Scherer, "Vocal measurement of emotion," in *Emotion: Theory, Research, and Experience*, vol. 4, R. Plutchik and H. Kellerman, Eds. San Diego: Academic Press, Inc., 1989, pp. 233-259.

[13] J. E. Cahn, "The generation of affect in synthesized speech," *Journal of the American voice I/O society*, vol. 8, pp. 1-19, 1990.

[14] L. Gong and C. Nass, "Does affect on computers matter?," Stanford University, Stanford, CA 2002.

[15] N. H. Frijda, "The laws of emotion," *American Psychologist*, vol. 43, pp. 349-358, 1988.

[16] L. Gong, C. Nass, C. Simard, and Y. Takhteyev, "When non-human is better than semi-human: Consistency in speech interfaces.," in *Usability evaluation and interface design: Cognitive engineering, intelligent agents, and virtual reality*, M. J. Smith, G. Salvendy, D. Harris, and R. Koubek, Eds. Mahwah, NJ: Lawrence Erlbaum Associates., 2001, pp. 1558-1562.

[17] M. Engleberg, J. A. Flora, and C. I. Nass, "AIDS knowledge: Effects of channel involvement and interpersonal communication," *Health Communication*, vol. 7, pp. 73-91, 1995.

[18] L. Gong, "Pairing media-captured human versus computer-synthesized humanoid faces and voices for talking heads: A consistency theory for interface agents," in *Communication*. Stanford, CA: Stanford University, 2001.

[19] P. R. Cohen, M. Johnston, D. McGee, S. L. Oviatt, J. Clow, and I. Smith, "The efficiency of multimodal interaction: a case study," in *Proceedings of the International Conference on Spoken Language*, 1998.

[20] E. André, T. Rist, S. v. Mulken, M. Klesen, and S. Baldes, "The Automated Design of Believable Dialogues for Animated Presentation Teams," in *Embodied Conversational Agents*, E. Churchill, Ed. Cambridge, MA: The MIT Press, 2000, pp. 220--255.

[21] S. E. Brennan and H. H. Clark, "Conceptual pacts and lexical choice in conversation," *Journal of experimental psychology: Learning, memory, and cognition*, vol. 22, pp. 1482-1493, 1996.

[22] S. Oviatt, "Ten myths of multimodal interaction," *Communications of the ACM*, vol. 42, pp. 74-81, 1999.

[23] R. Dawkins, *The selfish gene*, New ed. Oxford ; New York: Oxford University Press, 1989.

[24] C. D. Wickens, S. J. Mountford, and W. Schreiner, "Multiple resources, task-hemispheric integrity, and individual differences in time-sharing," *Human factors*, vol. 23, pp. 211-230, 1981.

[25]   C. D. Wickens, "The structure of attentional resources," in *Attention and performance VIII.*, R. Nickerson and R. Pew, Eds. New York, NY: Erlbaum, 1980.

[26]   S. Oviatt, A. DeAngeli, and K. Kuhn, "Integration and synchronization of input modes during multimodal human-computer interaction," in *Proceedings of Conference on Human Factors in Computing Systems (CHI '97)*. New York, NY: ACM Press, 1997, pp. 415-422.

[27]   J. M. Nye, "Human factors analysis of speech recognition systems," *Speech Technology*, vol. 1, pp. 50-57, 1982.

[28]   G. K. Poock, "Voice recognition boosts command terminal throughput," *Speech technology*, vol. 1, pp. 36-39, 1982.

[29]   R. I. Damper, M. A. Tranchant, and S. M. Lewis, "Speech versus keying in command and control: Effect of concurrent tasking.," *International Journal of Human-Computer Studies*, vol. 45, pp. 337-348., 1996.

[30]   R. E. Mayer, *Multimedia learning.* New York, NY: Cambridge University Press, 2001.

[31]   S. Brave, H. Ishii, and A. Dahley, "Tangible interfaces for remote collaboration and communication," presented at CSCW '98: Conference on Computer Supported Cooperative Work, 1998.

[32]   S. Bird, K. Maeda, X. Ma, H. Lee, B. Randall, and S. Zayat, "TableTrans, MultiTrans, InterTrans and TreeTrans: Diverse Tools Built on the Annotation Graph Toolkit," presented at Third International Conference on Language Resources and Evaluation (LREC), 2002.

[33]   C. Heeter, "Being there: The subjective experience of presence," *Presence: Teleoperators and Virtual Environment*, vol. 1, pp. 262-271, 1992.

[34]   F. Biocca, "The cyborg's dilemma: Progressive embodiment in virtual environments," *Journal of Computer-Mediated-Communication*, vol. 3, pp. Available: http://www.ascusc.org/jcmc/vol3/issue2/, 1997.

[35]   F. Biocca, B. Delaney, M. R. Levy, and et al., "Immersive virtual reality technology," in *LEA's communication series*. Hillsdale: Lawrence Erlbaum Associates Inc, 1995, pp. viii 401.

[36]   M. Lombard and T. B. Ditton, "At the heart of it all: The concept of presence," *Journal of Computer-Mediated-Communication*, vol. 3, pp. Available: http://www.ascusc.org/jcmc/vol3/issue2/, 1997.

[37]   M. Lombard, R. D. Reich, M. E. Grabe, C. Bracken, and T. B. Ditton, "Presence and television: The role of screen size," *Human Communication Research*, vol. 26, 2000.

[38]   K. Isbister and C. Nass, "Personality in conversational characters: Building better digital interaction partners using knowledge about human personality preferences and perceptions," presented at WECC Conference, Lake Tahoe, CA, 1998.

[39]   B. H. Detenber and B. Reeves, "A bio-informational theory of emotion: Motion and image size effects on viewers," *Journal of Communication*, vol. 46, pp. 66-84, 1996.

[40]   I. Altman and D. A. Taylor, *Social penetration: The development of interpersonal relationships.* New York, NY: Holt, Rinehart, and Winston, 1973.

[41]   C. D. Wickens, M. Vidulich, and D. Sandry-Garza, "Principles of S-C-R compatibility with spatial and verbal tasks: The role of display-control location and voice-interactive display-control interfacing.," *Human Factors Special Issue: Aviation psychology*, vol. 26, pp. 533-543., 1984.

[42]   M. T. Chi and W. G. Chase, "Effects of modality and similarity on context recall.," *Journal of Experimental Psychology*, vol. 96, pp. 219-222., 1972.

[43]   S. Sternberg, "High speed searching in human memory," *Science*, vol. 153, pp. 652-654, 1966.

[44]   H. P. Grice, *Intention and uncertainty.* London,: Oxford University Press, 1972.

Chapter 3

Voice User Interface Design for Novice and Experienced Users

James A. Larson
Intel Corporation

Key words: voice user interface, expert users, novice users

Abstract: With careful design and testing, voice application designers can develop efficient and enjoyable VoiceXML applications for both novice and experienced callers. VoiceXML lends itself to a system directed dialog for novice users, guiding them through the unfamiliar application and helping callers achieve their desired results. However, as callers become more experienced, they learn shortcuts to increase the pace of the dialog. Experienced users familiar with the structure and commands of the application can direct the application to perform actions quickly and efficiently using a type of mixed initiative dialog.

1.   INTRODUCTION

1.1   The novice-experienced user problem

Telephony applications enable callers to speak and listen to the computer using a telephone or cell phone in order to achieve computational tasks. Two general goals of most telephony applications are:
1. Enable anyone who can speak and listen to use telephony applications without previous training.
2. Enable all callers to perform tasks quickly and efficiently.

To achieve the first goal, many developers design telephony applications to be *application directed* (also called application-initiative, machine-directed, system directed, or directed dialogs)—the application leads the caller through the application by asking the caller questions to which the caller responds. With no previous training, callers who are not familiar with any telephony application are able to interact with the application.

However, users who frequently use the application may become impatient by listening to and answering the same questions in the same order each time they use the application. Average callers save time by volunteering the answers to the questions without waiting for the questions to be asked. Many average callers desire to take a more active role by leading the interaction with the application so that they can complete their tasks more quickly and efficiently. A *mixed initiative* telephony application enables callers to lead as well as be led by the application.

This paper describes how to develop telephony applications that can be both application directed and mixed initiative. Novice users answer detailed questions in response to verbal prompts to achieve their desired results, while average users speed up the interaction by volunteering an answer without waiting to listen to the entire prompt. Experienced users speak partial or full requests without answering several separate prompts.

1.2   VoiceXML

VoiceXML[1-4]   is a markup language for building telephony applications. VoiceXML can be thought of as the "HTML for telephony applications." By hiding many low-level details, developers use VoiceXML to create telephony applications by specifying high-level menus and forms rather than procedural programming code. Decreasing the programming time and effort enables developers to perform additional iterations of usability testing and design refinement. VoiceXML is lowering the entry barrier for creating telephony applications.

While VoiceXML makes it easy to create speech applications, it is difficult to create a good one. An HTML programmer easily learns how to write VoiceXML documents, but designing a usable VoiceXML application is still more of an art than a science. Most VoiceXML language manuals do not offer much advice for how to phrase a prompt, what to include in the grammar describing what a caller might say in response to a prompt, and what to do if the caller does not respond appropriately.

Figure 1 illustrates a fragment of a telephony application expressed using the VoiceXML language. This fragment illustrates a VoiceXML *form*—the equivalent of a paper form in which the caller enters a date consisting of *fields* containing values spoken by the caller and converted to text by a speech recognition engine. Each field has a *name* acting as a variable for the value of the field, a *prompt* that is presented to the caller as speech by either replaying a pre-recorded audio file or by a speech synthesis engine which converts a text string into spoken words, used by the speech recognition engine to convert spoken words into text. The speech recognition engine recognizes only words specified by the grammar and places the corresponding text string into the field name.

For example, in *Figure 1* the date form has three fields: month, day, and year. The month field has the prompt "What month?" that is converted to speech by a speech synthesizer and presented to the user. The user responds by speaking the name of one of the twelve months. Using the grammar that specifies the valid user responses to the prompt, the speech recognition converts the spoken month name into text, which is placed into the variable named "month."

```xml
<?xml version="1.0"?>
 <vxml version="2.0" xmlns = "http://www.w3.org/2001/vxml">
<form id = "date">
<field  name = "month">
    <prompt> What month? </prompt>
    <grammar root="month" version="1.0"
             type= "application/grammar+xml" >
       <rule id = "month">
          <one-of>
             <item>January</item>
             <item>February</item>
             <item>March</item>
             <item>April</item>
             <item>May</item>
             <item>June</item>
             <item>July</item>
             <item>August</item>
             <item>September</item>
             <item>October</item>
             <item>November</item>
             <item>December</item>
          </one-of>
       </rule>
    </grammar>
</field>
<field  name = "day">
    <prompt> What day of the month? </prompt>
    <grammar root="day" version = "1.0"
          type = "application/grammar+xml">
       <rule id = "day">
```

```
        <one-of>
            <item>one</item>
            <item>two</item>
            <!— items three through thirty omitted to save space —>
            <item>thirty-one</item>
        </one-of>
        </rule>
    </grammar>
</field>
<field name = "year">
    <prompt> What year? </prompt>
    <grammar root = "year" version = "1.0"
            type = "application/grammar+xml">
        <rule id = "year" >
            <one-of>
                <item>nineteen hundred</item>
                <item>nineteen hundred one</item>
                <!— items omitted to save space —>
                <item>two thousand ten</item>
            </one-of>
        </rule>
    </grammar>
</field>
</form>
</vxml>
```

Figure 1. Example of a VoiceXML dialog fragment

The form of *Figure 1* contains three fields—month, day, and year. VoiceXML processors use the *Form Interpretation Algorithm (FIA)* to sequence the fields for processing. The FIA selects the next field in the form whose field name has no value. In general, the FIA selects first the month field, then the day field, and finally the year field.

1.3   User classes

The caller's previous experience with speech applications is an important factor in the caller's ability to use a new speech application. At one extreme, a caller may be a *novice*—someone who has never used a speech interface. Novice callers may not know that they may barge-in before the end of a prompt, may not know how to ask for help, and may not know that they can skip over fields within a verbal form. At the other extreme, a caller may be *experienced*—someone who has used voice interfaces many times.

Experienced callers are able to leverage what they know about voice applications to explore and learn new voice applications. The experienced caller realizes that it is not necessary to listen to a complete prompt, it is possible to ask for help at any time just by saying "help," and may speak the field values for a voice form in any convenient order.

Because most callers have encountered a touch-tone menu system, they probably are one notch above a basic novice caller. However, many have never encountered voice-enabled applications and fall short of being experienced voice-application callers.

1.4   The three types of dialog styles

Figure 2 illustrates the typical flow of an application directed dialog. The application prompts the caller by asking a question or giving instructions and then waits for the caller to respond. The caller responds by speaking or pressing the buttons on a touch-tone phone. The application then performs the appropriate action, and the cycle begins again. When interpreted by a VoiceXML browser, the VoiceXML fragment of *Figure 1* might produce the application directed dialog illustrated in *Figure 2*.

Application:	What month?
Caller:	February
Application:	What day of the month?
Caller:	Twelve
Application:	What year?
Caller:	Nineteen ninety-seven

Figure 2. Example of an application directed dialog produced by the VoiceXML fragment in *Figure 1*

Application directed dialogs are easy to code and maintain. Many callers like application directed dialogs because they guide the caller through the application. The caller is not required to remember any commands or options (although with experience, callers do remember commands and options and use barge-in to speed up the dialog). Many callers have experienced application directed dialogs when using the touch-tone buttons on telephones. Most novice callers feel comfortable with application directed dialogs. On the negative side, callers may complain that the dialog is too structured and rigid, and takes too much time to complete. Some callers feel that the computer becomes their master and they become mere slaves to the computer.

With *user-directed dialogs* (also called user-initiative dialogs), the caller speaks to the application and instructs the application what to do. The caller speaks a request, the application performs the appropriate action and confirms the result to the caller, and then waits for the caller to speak the next request.   Then, the cycle starts again.   A user-directed dialog is illustrated in *Figure 3*.

Caller: Set month to February
Application: Month is February
Caller: Set day to twelve
Application: Day is twelve
Caller   Set year to nineteen ninety-seven
Application   Year is nineteen ninety-seven

Figure 3. Example of a user-directed dialog

The caller "drives" the dialog by initiating each dialog segment without explicit prompts.   User-directed dialogs generally require the caller to remember the names of commands and parameters.   While this is seldom a problem for an experienced caller, it may be problematic for a novice caller. This problem can be minimized with carefully designed help messages or a cue card listing the commands that the caller can carry in his wallet or her purse. After learning the command set, callers generally like user-directed dialogs because callers do not have to listen to lengthy menus. They feel in control of the application.

Mixed-initiative dialogs are a mixture of application directed and user-directed dialogs. *Figure 4* illustrates an application directed dialog.

Application: What month?
Caller: February twelve nineteen ninety-seven

Figure 4. A type of mixed initiative dialog in which the user takes the initiative to enter more data than was requested

Some callers become confused when they first encounter a mixed initiative dialog because they do not know what to do or when to barge-in. Perhaps this is because many callers are already familiar with application directed dialogs, especially touch-tone based applications, and have little experience with mixed initiative dialogs. Mixed-initiative dialogs feels more natural to most callers after they pass through an initial learning period.   On the negative side, mixed initiative dialogs can be more time-consuming to build, test, and maintain and may be more compute intensive.

2. DEVELOPING VOICE USER INTERFACES

The general process for developing a voice application is similar to the process for developing general application software. The steps are:

- Identify the application by interviewing prospective callers to identify their needs.
- Select the application to be developed and marketed.
- Develop usage scenarios and create a conceptual model of how the user will access the application.
- Develop the application.
- Test the application iteratively to refine the user interface.

However, there are some unique tasks that must be performed when developing voice user interfaces, including specifying prompt messages to solicit information from the caller, writing grammars to describe the words and phrases a caller may speak in response prompts, and writing error handlers to help the caller resolve problems that occur when the speech recognition engine fails to recognize the user utterance.

Several guidelines for developing voice user interfaces will be described, along with examples of how to implement the guidelines using the most recent version of VoiceXML 2.0. The guidelines are grouped into three clusters:

- Guidelines for voice user interfaces for novice users—First time callers who need to be guided through the application
- Guidelines for voice user interfaces for average users—Callers who have used the voice application several times and want to speed up the pace of the interaction
- Guidelines for voice user interfaces for experienced users—Callers who are very familiar with the application and do not need to be guided through the application.

See [5] for additional human-factors guidelines for speech applications.

3. GUIDELINES FOR VOICE USER INTERFACES FOR NOVICE USERS

These guidelines are designed for developing voice user interfaces for novice users who need to be guided through the application. Developers use these guidelines to design system directed dialogs that can easily be implemented in VoiceXML 2.0. The guidelines are:

- Match the organization of the voice user interface to the caller's perspective

- Guide the caller.
- Use error handlers to provide help to the caller.
- Provide progressive assistance.

3.1 Match the organization of the voice user interface to the caller's perspective

Callers frequently use a voice user interface to achieve specific results. For example, callers access a voice mail system to review and possibly create and send voice mail messages. The best way to organize a voice user interface is by a task flow that matches the sequence of tasks normally performed by the user. For example, the caller first reviews a list of received messages, selects a message for review, and may then record, edit and send a response. The voice user interface should be designed to facilitate this typical sequence of tasks.

In North America, callers usually say the date in month-day-year sequence. The VoiceXML fragment in *Figure 1* illustrates how a voice user interface asks for date information in the same sequence that North American callers usually write dates. Europeans frequently write dates in the sequence of day-month-year. For European callers, designers should consider switching the position of the month and day fields so that the user interface more closely matches how Europeans write dates.

3.2 Guide the caller

Most callers have experienced touch-tone applications which are generally of the form "for accounting, press one; for sales, press two; ..." Callers who are not familiar with the application find these system-directed dialogs an easy and natural way to interact with a voice over a telephone or cell phone despite the cognitive task of mapping the user's request to pressing a numbered key on a telephone or cell phone keypad. Currently, many callers have never experienced a user-directed voice dialog and will not know what to do if the voice application asks an open-ended question, such as "What would you like to do next?" (This situation may change as more users begin to experience mixed initiative dialogs.)

Designers should create applications that guide the novice caller towards speaking responses that the speech recognition engine. It is much better to use "suggestive" prompts rather than require the user to memorize and recall words.

Phrase each question to solicit a simple answer. Either enumerate the words that the user may speak in response to the question, such as "How do you want to travel? By air, boat or car," or identify a class of words well-known to the user, such as "Which day of the month?" An experienced caller may speed up the dialog by barging-in during the question by speaking a response.

3.3 Use error handlers to provide help to the caller

Voice tutorials presented at the beginning of an application have not proven to be helpful to users. Users have difficulty remembering the details presented in voice tutorials. Also many users resent the time required to listen to them. Instead of presenting wordy tutorials, developers should provide just-in-time help. When the user becomes confused and does not know how to respond, the user asks for help. Help is provided in a short verbal message to the user expressed in the context of the user's current point in the dialog. If the user fails to respond to a question or responds with a word not recognized by the speech recognition engine, present a help message to the caller explaining appropriate responses.

When errors occur the application responds according to instructions specified by the dialog designer in *event handlers* that are special snippets of VoiceXML code especially designed to help users resolve errors. VoiceXML detects several types of events, including:

Help. The caller has explicitly asked for help. Provide a more detailed explanation of what the user should say.

Noinput. The caller did not respond to a prompt before the timeout. Either the caller did not understand the prompt or does not know how to answer the question. Consider telling the caller "I didn't hear you," and rephrase the question using different wording.

Nomatch. The caller has uttered a word or phrase that is not recognized by the speech recognition system. Consider telling the caller "I didn't understand you." Rephrase the question and enumerate the possible answers.

Figure 5 illustrates event handlers for assisting users when they ask for help or encounter noinput or nomatch events. Event handlers typically use the <catch> tag to intercept the event. In these examples, the user is prompted to try again. When no value has been placed into the month field, the FIA continues to solicit a value for the month field.

```
<?xml version="1.0"?>
 <vxml version="2.0" xmlns = "http://www.w3.org/2001/vxml">

<form id = "date">
<field  name = "month">
```

```
<prompt count = "1"> What month? </prompt>
<catch event = "nomatch">
    <prompt>
        I did not understand you.  Which month of the year?
    </prompt>
</catch>
<catch event = "noinput">
    <prompt>
        I did not hear you.  Which month of the year?
    </prompt>
</catch>
<catch event ="help">
    <prompt>
        Which month of the year? For example, January.
    </prompt>
</catch>
<grammar root = "month"
        type = "application/grammar+xml" version = "1.0">
    <rule id = "month">
        <one-of>
            <item>January</item>
            <!— items omitted to save space —>
            <item>December</item>
        </one-of>
        </rule>
    </grammar>
</field>
</form>
</vxml>
```

Figure 5. Example event handlers for assisting users in resolving errors

3.4   Provide progressive assistance

Sometimes a simple help message is not enough—the caller fails to respond, responds incorrectly, or asks for additional help. In these situations, reveal additional information and instructions to the caller each time the caller fails to respond correctly. Designers frequently write levels of help messages to provide additional assistance for each level. *Figure 6* and *Figure 7* illustrate four levels of progressive assistance:

Level 1—Present a short prompt asking the caller to respond.
Level 2—Present a short description of what the caller should say.

Level 3—Present an example of what the caller should do.

Level 4—Offer to present short segments of a verbal tutorial to the caller or transfer the caller to a human operator to resolve the caller's problem.

If for any reason a value is not inserted into the month field, the FIA attempts to solicit the missing value from the user. After each failure, the prompt count is incremented by one, and the next prompt wording is presented to the user.

```
<?xml version="1.0"?>
<vxml version="2.0" xmlns = "http://www.w3.org/2001/vxml">

<form id = "date">
<field  name = "month">
   <prompt count = "1"> What month? </prompt>
   <catch event = "help nomatch noinput" count = "2">
      <prompt>Which month of the year?  </prompt>
   </catch>
   <catch event = "help nomatch noinput" count = "3">
      <prompt>
            Which month of the year?  For example, January.
      </prompt>
   </catch>
   <catch event = "help nomatch noinput" count = "4">
      <throw event = "transfer"/>
   </catch>
</field>
<catch event="transfer">
   <prompt> Transferring.  Please hold. </prompt>
   <!— goto code fragment that transfers user —>
   <exit/>
</catch>

<grammar root = "month" version = "1.0"
      type = "application/grammar+xml">
   <rule id = "month">
     <one-of>
        <item>January</item>
        <!— items omitted to save space —>
        <item>December</item>
     </one-of>
     </rule>
</grammar>
```

```
</form>
</vxml>
```
Figure 6. Example of four levels of progressive assistance

Application:	What month?
Caller:	Huh?
Application:	What month of the year?
Caller:	Uh, aa. . .
Application:	What month of the year? For example, January.
Caller:	Aa...
Application:	Transferring, please hold.

Figure 7. Dialog illustrating progressive assistance

Callers will tolerate only a limited number of failures before they give up and abandon the application. The application should connect the caller to a human operator before this happens. Only user testing will determine the approximate number of caller failures before the caller gives up.

As callers use the system and listen to the short help messages, they will gradually learn how to use that portion of the voice application. The more the caller uses the voice application, the more expertise the caller obtains. This type of incremental learning enables the user to progress from novice to expert level at the user's own rate. The user only learns about the portions of the application that the caller frequently uses. If the expert user forgets a detail, the expert can easily ask for help.

4.   GUIDELINES FOR VOICE USER INTERFACES FOR AVERAGE USERS

Average callers may complain that application directed dialogs are too time-consuming, especially when callers must listen to prompt messages that they have heard many times before. When applied to a VoiceXML 2.0 application, guidelines will enable callers to accelerate their interaction so they can complete their desired tasks faster and easier. These guidelines are
– Enable barge-in
– Enable alternative utterances

4.1   Enable barge-in

Barge-in enables callers to interrupt and speak before the completion of a voice prompt. As soon as the caller speaks, the prompt stops. The caller will not hear the remainder of the prompt. For average callers who are familiar with the telephony application, barge-in increases the pace of interaction.

Barge-in speeds up a verbal conversation for experienced callers. However, barge-in is a double-edged sword. While barge-in increases the pace of interaction, callers may miss important information. Dialog designers should design prompts so that important information appears early in the prompt. *Figure 8* illustrates the same dialog as *Figure 2* except the caller is allowed to barge-in.

Application: What month?
Caller: February
Application: What day of....
Caller: (barges in) twelve
Application: What ...
Caller: (barges in) nineteen ninety-seven

Figure 8. Example dialog illustrating barge-in

4.2   Enable alternative utterances

When average callers barge-in, they may not hear the choices presented at the end of a prompt. Average callers may not remember the exact words and phrases and may utter synonyms instead. Application designers should include these synonyms in the grammar associated with the field containing the prompt. For example, *Figure 9* illustrates the grammar used in the day field of *Figure 1*. The grammar is extended to enable the caller say "first," "second," ... "thirty-first" in addition to "one," "two," ... "thirty-one."

```
<?xml version="1.0"?>
<vxml version="2.0" xmlns = "http://www.w3.org/2001/vxml">
<form id = "date">
   <field name = "day">
      <prompt> What day of the week? </prompt>
      <grammar root = "day" version = "1.0"
            type = "application/grammar+xml">
         <rule id = "day">
           <one-of>
             <item>one</item>
             <item>two</item>
             <!— items three through thirty omitted to save space —>
             <item>thirty-one</item>
             <item> <tag>$.day = "one"</tag>first</item>
             <item> <tag>$.day = "two"</tag>second</item>
```

```
        <!— items three through thirty omitted to save space —>
        <item><tag>$.day="thirty-one"</tag> thirty-first</item>
      </one-of>
    </rule>
  </grammar>
</field>
</form>
</vxml>
```

Figure 9. Grammar from the day field in *Figure 1* extended to enable the caller to say both ordinal and cardinal numbers.

Semantic interpretation tags enable a text string to be substituted for words spoken by the caller. In the example above, "one" is substituted for "first," "two" is substituted for "second," and so on.

During user testing, developers should record alternate words and synonyms spoken by callers in response to prompts and consider adding these words to the grammar associated with the field containing the prompt.

Alternative utterances enable callers to speak words not included in the prompts as well as words included in the prompts but not heard when the caller barges-in. Enabling the caller to speak synonyms makes the dialog more flexible and results in fewer nomatch events and requests for help by the caller. However, larger grammars may slow the speech recognition engine, which may result in increased latency for the application.

5.   GUIDELINES FOR USER INTERFACES FOR EXPERIENCED USERS

Experienced users are familiar with the structure and content of the application. They need shortcuts that accelerate the interaction. The following guidelines result in enhancements to a system directed VoiceXML application enabling it to support a type of mixed initiative dialog:
– Enable task switching
– Enable single utterance for multiple fields
– Enable out-of-sequence data entry
– Prompt for missing parameters
– Resolve overlapping grammars

5.1 Enable task switching

Many visual applications contain a navigation bar. Clicking a word or icon on the navigation bar causes the user to jump to another document or application. The VoiceXML equivalent of a navigation bar is called a *root document*. A *root document* acts as an index to other verbal documents and applications. The root document presents callers with a verbal menu of universal commands that the caller can speak at any time to be automatically transferred the corresponding application. The designer includes the name of each target application as a grammar in the <link> tag. For example, if the dialog designer includes "deposit" as a link in the root document, then whenever a caller says "deposit," the caller is transferred immediately to the deposit document.

Novice callers listen to a list of services before selecting and speaking the name of the desired application. Experienced callers simply say the name of the desired application.

Figure 10 illustrates a fragment of a root document that enables the caller to select from among several verbal forms: date, address, and credit card. The caller may say "date," "address," or "credit card" at any time to be transferred to the corresponding application.

```
<initial>
   <prompt>
        Welcome to your reservation profile.
        Do you want to update your arrival date, address, or credit card?
   </prompt>
   <link next="#date1">
           <grammar root = "day" version = "1.0"
                 type = "application/grammar+xml">
                <rule id = "day"> <item> arrival date </item> </rule>
           </grammar>
        </link>

   <link next="#address1">
           <grammar root = "address" version = "1.0"
                 type = "application/grammar+xml">
                <rule id = "address"> <item> address </item> </rule>
           </grammar>
        </link>
```

```
<link next="#card1">
      <grammar root = "card" version = "1.0"
            type = "application/grammar+xml">
            <rule id = "card"> <item> credit card </item>  </rule>
      </grammar>
   </link>
</initial>
```

Figure 10. Transfer to another application

5.2   Enable single utterance for multiple fields

Callers can bypass a prompt by speaking multiple words in the same
utterance.   A form-level grammar is required to do this.   A *form-level
grammar* contains grammar rules for how grammars for individual fields
(called *field-level grammars*) may be combined and sequenced within a
single utterance. For example, the form-level grammar highlighted below in
Figure 11 enables an American caller to say "January thirteen two thousand
four" in a single utterance in response to the prompt, "What date?" If the
caller's utterance matches the entire sequence, then all fields receive their
respective values.   If a user does not respond to the form-level prompt
(which is only presented once, when the FIA first enters the form) before the
timeout period, then the FIA will visit each individual field, presenting its
prompt and listening for words in each field-level grammar.

```
<form id = "date">
<initial>
   <prompt> What date?> </prompt>
</initial>
   <grammar root = "American-date" version = "1.0"
            type = "application/grammar+xml">
      <!— the following is a form-level grammar —>
      <rule id = "American_date">
         <ruleref name= "#month">
         <ruleref name= "#day">
         <ruleref name= "#year">
      </rule>
      <!— the following are field-level grammars —>
      <rule id = "month">
         <one-of>
            <item>January</item>
            <!— February through November omitted to save space —>
```

```
            <item>December</item>
         </one-of>
      </rule>

      <rule id = "day">
         <one-of>
            <item>one</item>
            <item>two</item>
            <!— items three through thirty omitted to save space —>
            <item>thirty-one</item>
         </one-of>
      </rule>

      <rule id = "year">
         <one-of>
            <item>nineteen hundred</item>
            <item>nineteen hundred one</item>
            <!— items omitted to save space —>
            <item>two thousand two</item>
         </one-of>
        </rule>
     </grammar>
<field name = "month">
  ...
<field name = "day" >
  ...
<field name = "year">
...
</form>
```

Figure 11. Example form-level grammar

By specifying multiple form-level grammar rules as illustrated in *Figure 12*, designers enable callers to utter alternative sequences of words. For example, the following form-level grammar rules enable an American caller to say "January thirteen, two thousand two," and enable a European caller to say "Thirteen January, two thousand two."

```
<rule id = "date">
  <one-of>
      <ruleref name = "#American_date">
      <ruleref name = "#European_date">
  </one-of>
<rule id = "American_date">
   <ruleref name= "#month">
   <ruleref name= "#day">
   <ruleref name= "#year">
</rule>
<rule id = "European_date">
   <ruleref name= "#day">
   <ruleref name= "#month">
   <ruleref name= "#year">
</rule>
```

Figure 12. Example of a complex form-level grammar enabling multiple sequences of field-level grammars

5.3   Enable out-of-sequence data entry

If a field's grammar is defined at the form level, then the grammar associated with the field is active throughout the entire form—not just the field in which the grammar is specified. The speech recognition engine listens for words in all active grammars and places recognized words into the appropriate field variables. This increases the flexibility of the dialog document by enabling the caller to speak the names of the values in any order and have those values placed into the proper fields, as illustrated in *Figure 13*.

Application:	What date?
Caller:	(no response)
Application:	What month?
Caller:	Twelfth
Application:	What month?
Caller:	February
Application:	What year?

Caller: Nineteen ninety-seven

Figure 13. Example dialog in which the user speaks the values out of sequence

5.4   Prompt for missing parameters

Suppose a caller first speaks the month and day and is then silent for the year. The FIA will prompt the caller for values for unvisited fields—in this case, the Year field. The resulting dialog is illustrated in *Figure 14*.

Application: What date?
Caller: February twelfth
Application: What year?
Caller: Nineteen ninety-seven

Figure 14. Example dialog in which the user omits a value and is prompted to supply the missing value

The FIA sequences through the empty fields of a form one at a time, prompting the caller for values. The FIA sets a guard variable associated with each form field when the caller supplies a value for that field. If the caller enters a value out of sequence, the FIA accepts that value and marks the field's guard variable. The FIA cycles through the form again and again until all guard variables are marked—and all of the fields have values.

Developers specify form-level prompts to encourage the caller to respond with multiple parameters. Developers specify field-level prompts to solicit individual parameters not spoken in response to the form level prompt.

5.5   Resolve overlapping grammars

Suppose the caller has two types of accounts—checking and savings. The transfer form first asks for the source account and then asks for the target account. Suppose further that the caller answers the first prompt by saying "checking." Because "checking" is a value for both the source_account and the target_account, it is not clear whether the caller means that "checking" is intended to be the source or the target. This can be resolved by adding the words "to" and "from" to the grammar. The caller speaks the words "to" and "from" to indicate whether "checking" is the source or target. Specifically, if the caller says, "to checking," then the "checking" becomes the value of target_account. However, if the caller says "from checking," then "checking" becomes the value of the source_account. The <tag> element contains semantic interpretation instructions that specify which variable, source or target, should receive the value "checking." As illustrated in *Figure 15,* the semantic interpretation that assigns the value "checking" to target_account is attached to the grammar rule containing the word "to," while the semantic attachment that assigns the value "checking" to source_account is attached to the grammar rule containing the word "from."

```
<rule id = "source_account">
from
<one-of>
   <item> <tag>$.source_account="savings" </tag> savings </item>
   <item><tag>$.source_account="checking"</tag>checking </item>
</one-of>
</rule>
<rule id = "target_account">
   to
<one-of>
   <item> <tag> $.target_account="savings" </tag> savings </item>
   <item> <tag>$.target_account="checking"</tag>checking </item>
</one-of>
</rule>
```

Figure 15. Overlapping grammars resolved by semantic interpretation commands

6.   ADVANCED TECHNIQUES

To understand a caller's utterance, VoiceXML and the underlying speech recognition system use information from the following sources:
−   The caller's utterance
−   Syntactic information encoded within the grammar
−   Tags embedded into the grammar that contains semantic processing instructions for extracting and translating words from the user's utterance.

Additional information can be used to improve the understanding of what the caller says. This information can be extracted from the utterances of typical users, and the context in which the caller's utterance appears.

6.1   Statistical techniques

Two statistical techniques that can be used with VoiceXML are N-grams and classifiers.

A large vocabulary of words may be represented by N-grams. *N-grams* encode sequences of words that appear together in spoken languages such as English, Spanish, or Chinese restricted to a specific domain such as medical, legal, or scientific area. If N=2, then pairs of words are used to describe utterances in the domain. If N=3, then triples of words are used. To create an N-gram language model, the developer collects large samples of text from the specific domain. Statistical algorithms construct the collection of N-grams and their frequencies within the text samples and represent the language model in a data structure that can be searched quickly. Rather than trying to write a grammar for a large collection of user utterances, developers can generate and use an N-gram language model.

Classifiers have long been used in information storage and retrieval applications to classify documents into categories or topics for easy retrieval. Classifiers have also been used in vision applications to categorize—sort graphical objects—based on the color or visual patterns. AT&T has introduced a speech classification system called How May I Help You (HMIHY) [6] that applies classification technology to convert a caller's initial request into one of several topics, and routes the call accordingly.

Unlike typical speech dialog systems where callers must navigate through menu choices by saying prespecified words, HMIHY callers simply say what they want. The HMIHY system recognizes key words and phrases and routes the call to a category specific subsystem, either another artificial agent or a human operator. Classifiers enable speakers to verbalize a request in their own words rather than select prespecified words from menu hierarchies. This shifts the burden from callers to the computer. Callers find the system much easier to use than traditional conversational speech systems because they spend less time getting what they need.

No longer must a developer structure the menu hierarchy and write all of the prompts, grammars, and error handlers. But the developer must pay a price. The developer must (1) collect large corpora of typical caller utterances, (2) annotate each with the appropriate topic, and (3) train the classifier to *classify* (match) caller utterances to topics. Furthermore, if the topics requested by callers change, then the whole process may need to be repeated.

6.2 Context

Grammars with embedded tags use context within the caller's utterance to extract and translate words. Understanding a caller's utterance can be improved by using additional sources of context, including:

Caller profile which contains the information about the caller's interest and previous activities that may be useful in understanding the caller's current requests. For Example, if the caller profile indicates that the caller is a farmer, then the noun "run" could be interpreted as a holding area for livestock, such as a chicken run. On the other hand, if the caller profile indicates that the caller is interested in athletic events, then the word "run" could be interpreted as a race.

Previous utterances may provide hints and clues for the interpretation of a user's utterance. For example, If the caller spoke about chickens in the previous utterance, the word "run" probably refers to a chick run rather than an event for athletics.

Advanced artificial intelligence algorithms can replace a simple VoiceXML grammar to provide an improved understanding of a user's utterance. The use of caller profiles and context is an ongoing research topic that will provide additional power to VoiceXML.

7.   ITERATIVE TESTING

Coding voice applications for both novice and experienced callers is easy. Specifying he right prompts, grammars, and event handlers is difficult. Many designers use iterative usability testing—a repeated cycle in which users test the system and designers refine prompts, grammars and event handlers.

As the number of words and phrases in a grammar grows, more time is required by the speech recognition engine to recognize the words spoken by the user. Developers manage the trade-off between vocabulary size and the number of nomatch events by conducting usability tests to measure the speed of the speech recognition engine and the number of nomatch events. Developers attempt to minimize both by fine-tuning the prompt wordings and grammars. In addition, universal commands may cause performance problems because the speech recognition engine must also consider universal commands during each recognition phase. Developers try to minimize the number of universal commands to increase the recognition engine's response time, as well as decrease the number of commands that an experienced user must remember.

During each testing phase the developers carefully analyse the dialog. For each field in which the caller asks for help or causes a nomatch or noinput event, consider revising the prompt to be more specific and consider additional event handlers. For each field in which a nomatch event occurs, consider adding the word spoken by the caller to the grammar for the field.

Developers use the <log> tag to record timestamped events and values to a history log. A software log analysis application summarizes and calculates performance measurements. *Performance measurements* are objective measurements of how many actions the caller is able to complete in a specified period of time and how many times a caller attempted to perform an action without success. Without performance measurements, it is difficult to know if code changes actually improve performance.

Developers interview callers after each test to collect caller preference measurements. *Preference measurements* (sometimes called usability measurements) are subjective measurements of how users like various aspects of the voice application. Preference measurements indicate how likely a caller is to use the voice application again.

8. SUMMARY

It is easy to learn how to use VoiceXML syntax to create a working voice application, but effort is required to develop a voice application that is both efficient and enjoyable for novice, average, and experienced users. Novice users are presented with a system directed dialog that guides them through the application and helps them achieve the desired goals. By extending grammars and enabling barge-in, average callers can increase the pace of the dialog. By using form-level grammars and encouraging callers to take a more active role in the dialog, experienced callers direct the application to achieve the desired results using a type of mixed initiative dialog. Finally, iterative testing and user interface refinement are necessary for developing efficient and enjoyable voice applications.

ACKNOWLEDGEMENTS:

The author acknowledges the many contributors to the VoiceXML language. Thanks first to the founders of the VoiceXML Forum who specified VoiceXML 1.0, and then to the members of the World Wide Web Consortium who specified VoiceXML 2.0.

REFERENCES

[1] B. Edgar, *VoiceXML: The Telephony-enabled Web*. New York: CMP Books, 2001.
[2] E. A. Andersson, S. Breitenbach, T. Burd, N. Chidambaram, P. Houle, D. Newsome, X. Tang, and X. Zhu, *Early Adopter VoiceXML*. Birmingham, UK: Wrox Press, 2001.
[3] R. Beasley, K. M. Farley, J. O'Reilly, L. Squire, and K. Farley, *Voice Application Development with VoiceXML*: Sams, 2002.
[4] J. A. Larson, *VoiceXML: Introduction to developing speech applications*. Upper Saddle River New Jersey: Prentice Hall, 2002.
[5] B. Balentine and D. Morgan, *How to build a speech recognition application*. San Ramon, California: Enterprise Integration Group, 1999.
[6] ATT, "How May I Help You?" http://www.research.att.com/~jwright/hmihy/,

Chapter 4

Designing Error Recovery Dialogs
Handling misrecognition and misunderstanding in practical human-computer dialogs

Morena Danieli
Loquendo-Vocal Technologies

Key words: Miscommunication, human-machine misunderstanding, error recovery, misrecognition.

Abstract: The focus of this chapter is on the design of error recovery dialogs in oral human-machine systems. We will investigate on two related issues: on the one hand, how to recognize user's detection of errors by the artificial agent, on the other one how to avoid frustrating error recovery subdialogs. Although many of the possible choices at the design level depend on the capabilities of the dialog system, we will show how a careful design can be provided even for simple spoken dialog systems.

1.   INTRODUCTION

Speech recognition technologies have dramatically improved during the last decade, yet oral human-computer communication is still error prone. The occurrence of various kinds of miscommunication phenomena is an intrinsic feature not only of complex, and nearly conversational, laboratory prototypes, but also of practical human-machine dialog systems.

Miscommunication is often originated by the errors of the automatic speech recognition engines, but sometimes it is a consequence of 'misleading' linguistic behavior of human users who may be either unfamiliar or uncooperative with spoken language systems. It has been a goal of researchers in spoken dialog for many years to provide a robust basis for dealing with communication failures. Most of the studies on this subject share the underlying assumption that miscommunication in face-to-face dialog is a pervasive phenomenon.

At present, the capabilities of most practical dialog systems are not sophisticated enough to implement human-like conversational skills, and their usability can be greatly reduced by the occurrence of various kinds of miscommunication. The sense of frustration we may experience while using some spoken dialog applications is often due to poor error recovery management.

Designing effective error recovery strategies is thus an important factor of users' acceptance of practical dialog applications. It is clear that the design of error recovery strategies may depend on the underlying capabilities of different dialog systems: if a given dialog manager supports the updating of focus structures, or the maintenance of context structures, then the dialog designer can rely on powerful mechanisms for detecting miscommunication phenomena and repairing their disruptive consequences. Nevertheless, in this chapter we will argue that also the design of simpler, practical spoken dialog applications should rely on a set of best practice principles, specifically devoted to dealing with misperception, misrecognition, and misunderstanding of oral discourse.

This chapter has two goals: first, we would like to illustrate the different kinds of miscommunication phenomena that may occur while using a speech-based system. Second, we will suggest that the occurrences of human-computer miscommunication can be prevented and repaired by applying some principled dialog design strategies.

The chapter is organized as follows: The next section will provide some introductory remarks for a better understanding of the most relevant aspects of human-machine misunderstanding. Section 3 introduces a classification of the most common typologies of misunderstanding on the basis of classificatory parameters such as which agent (human or machine) originated the error, and at which level of analysis the error occurred. This classification will be helpful for distinguishing user-initiated from system-initiated repairs, and for providing dialog design principles for dealing with each category. In Section 4, we approach the issue of designing error recovery dialogs by providing examples and guidelines for "preventing, detecting and repairing human-machine miscommunication"[1]. Should the reader be interested in learning more on the present issue, a list of relevant references is provided in the last section of the chapter.

[1] Paraphrasing the title of a workshop held during the 1996 Annual Conference of the American Association for Artificial Intelligence in Portland, Oregon [1].

2. HUMAN-MACHINE MISCOMMUNICATION

2.1 Human-human (mis-)communication

Before approaching the issues related to miscommunication in human-machine interaction, we would like to discuss human communication and miscommunication. In fact, we want to illustrate the conceptual framework that inspires our analysis, i.e. the theory of speech acts, introduced by John L. Austin [2] in the mid-fifties. This well-known theory constituted a change in the study of language: originally it was a reaction to the inadequacies of the neo-positivistic restrictions to the classes of sentences worth to be philosophically investigated In the neo-positivistic view, only the propositions that can be true or false are objects of philosophical investigation. On the contrary, Austin showed that most of the social uses of language cannot be explained in terms of truth values, but they can be accounted for in terms of contextual appropriateness. For example, sentences containing verbs such as "marry" or "promise" if appropriately uttered constitute the execution of actions.

Austin's intuitions about the strict relationships between communication and (physical) actions had a huge impact in several fields, from philosophy of language [3, 4] to linguistics [5] from psychology of language [6] to artificial intelligence.

The basic ideas of speech acts theory are widespread in the research on natural language and dialog processing since the publication of Winograd [7] and Allen and Perrault [8]. The central issue of Austin's proposal is the relationship between speech and action. This connection is complex because of the interplay between communicative intentions and situational contexts. The intentions underlying humans' verbal and non-verbal behavior can modify the context where actions are situated, and the evolving nature of communication can modify humans' intentions about actions to be performed. The complexity of this connection is well illustrated in recent psychological work on situated communication such as [9]. These authors claim that actions situated in the real world can both aid and impair communication, given that the intentional actions of human agents can modify the situational context. In addition, ongoing communication can modify the agents' intentions about actions. Finally, they take into account a third element, i.e. the fact that "the state of the physical world influences the possibility of performing actions and communicative acts". Roughly speaking, on the basis of speech acts theory and its further elaboration in different disciplines of communication, we can interpret communication as a *situated process* where speakers' communicative behavior is *action* ruled by
- Speaker's perception of the social and physical environment,

- Speaker's perception of other's speakers intentions,
- Speaker's knowledge about the goal s/he wants to achieve in the communication.

If we take as conceptual background the view that speech *is* (also) action, conversely we can interpret failure of communication as action failure. In particular, we will refer to the operative definition of *communication failure* proposed by Traum and Dillenbourg [10], i.e.

> "miscommunication can be viewed as instances of action failure (when the speaker fails to produce the intended effect), misperception (when the hearer cannot recognize what the speaker intended to communicate), or both" (p. 37).

If we take seriously the interplay between communication and action, we can investigate the case of communication failure on the basis of three dimensions of the miscommunication phenomenon, i.e.

- The role played by (physical) action failure and misperception,
- The failure of intentionality
- The influence of the state of the (physical) world on the success of communicative acts.

Before moving to the application of this conceptual framework to the special case of human-computer miscommunication, we would like to recall that in human-human communication the phenomena related to misunderstanding are widespread. Several scholars have studied communication failures since the early nineties: Susan McRoy [1], among others, showed that the ability to deal with miscommunication is central to the study of interpersonal communication. In other words, in human-human communication misunderstanding, mishearing, and misconceptions are not the exceptions but the rule. Yet, most of the times humans effectively communicate!

2.2   Human-machine miscommunication

Practitioners of human-computer natural language interface design tend to identify in the system most of the potential causes of human-machine miscommunication. In particular, when the conversation between human and machine is oral, recognition errors are considered the first cause of the degradation of the quality of the dialog. We believe that this impression is largely true, but that system misperception is just one of the causes of failure in the communication process. A neglected potential cause of miscommunication can be ascribed to the speaker's behavior, as we are going to explain in the next paragraph.

In   human-machine   oral   interactions,   the   occurrence   of miscommunication is always characterized by an inadequacy in the transmission of intentions due to action failure and/or misperception.

In the case of human-machine miscommunication the role that the physical environment plays in communication between humans is played by the status of the communication channel. Moreover, we have to add a further feature related to the fact that some elements of the communication context which are relevant for the achievement of the practical goal of the interaction, can become unavailable during the course of the interaction. For example, if a practical dialog system has to access external resources for providing the user with retrieved information, communication failures may occur when such resources are not available. We will refer to this situation by using the label "incompleteness" of the resources needed to accomplish the interaction task. These three different, yet inter-related, potential causes of human-machine miscommunication can be illustrated by considering the scheme in *Figure 1*.

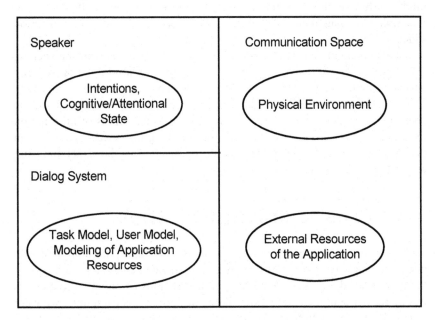

Figure 1. Speaker, dialog system and communication space

In the scheme we can see that the speaker and the dialog system have different levels of access to the COMMUNICATION SPACE, on the right of the scheme. For the dialog system this space is represented by the set of external resources it can access; for the speaker, the COMMUNICATION SPACE is the physical environment s/he can perceive. The figure also shows the different cognitive models of speaker and system: as we could expect, there is a cognitive discrepancy between the two actors of the interaction, but notice that the dialog system is the only one that can access the application resources needed to accomplish the interaction goal. In this sense, it can monitor both the *discourse state* and an important feature of the communication space such as the availability of the sources of information to be provided to the users.

When the communication process goes smoothly, the speaker and the system can complete the interaction task by sharing the pieces of information necessary and sufficient for providing the user with the required information or/and with the desired actions. However, when this process is affected by miscommunication, the resulting action failure is often due to the user's unawareness of the discourse state.

This lack of awareness can be due to insufficient knowledge about the kind of information the system is going to ask for completing the task, or to incomplete management of the relevant features of the communication space.

Other potential causes of misleading behavior on the part of the speaker are related to an excessive cognitive load induced by a poor dialog strategy or poor quality of one or more modules of the dialog system. This may happen, for example, when the implemented dialog strategy asks the speakers to provide, in the same dialog turn, different pieces of information that are not meaningfully related, or when poor speech recognition performance requires the user to proceed by uttering the exact phrasing suggested by the system.

3.   KINDS OF MISCOMMUNICATION

While interacting with a spoken dialog system, miscommunication phenomena can be due both to errors of the artificial agent, and to errors of the human speaker. As we have seen in the previous paragraph, these errors can be further complicated by poor dialog design. In this paragraph, we want to classify the most frequent kinds of communication errors that may occur in practical dialog domains.

Since the early nineties, human-machine practical dialog has been applied to a variety of telecommunication domains, including automation of call centers, directory assistance, transport information, acquisition of delivery orders, and home banking. Although is very difficult to generalize, from the analysis of some assessment studies, we can try to design an operational classification of different kinds of miscommunication phenomena, which we illustrate in *Table 1*. The classification is not complete because of the difficulty in classifying in a principled way the large variety of linguistic behavior of real users of practical dialog systems. Moreover, while a lot of practical dialog systems are being developed in different countries, researchers working in the area of spoken dialog design have little data concerning the evaluation of how the systems perform in real field conditions[2]. Nevertheless, this classification can be useful as a general scheme to be referred to when designing a dialog strategy for a new practical dialog application.

This classification scheme interprets miscommunication on the basis of the action failure paradigm we introduced above. In the first column of the table the potential causes of miscommunication are reported. We can observe that the different levels of causes vary along a *continuum*: at the extremes of that there are errors due to inadequacies of both system and user concerning the knowledge of the dialog state (system, bottom of the table) and structure of the task (top of the table).

In the second column of the table the different types of action failures that correspond to each potential cause are reported. The third column refers to the origin of the cause of failure: whenever it was possible, plausible reasons of the failure are identified. This inventory is not exhaustive: we have identified some aspects behind the behavior of both user and system that can be studied from the point of view of spoken dialog design.

It is worth noticing that two out of five potential causes of miscommunication can be ascribed to users' behavior. For example, the inattentive behavior of the speaker may produce errors that are situated at different levels of analysis (from pronunciation errors to semantically incomplete sentences). The potential reason of inattentive behavior may be identified in the cognitive load involved in using spoken language systems. Our suggestions will be about designing dialog strategies that take that fact into account.

---

[2] The DARPA Communicator project constitutes an exception. In June of 2000 an experimental data collection was conducted with nine DARPA Communicator systems. The paper [11] describes the application of the PARADISE evaluation framework to 662 dialogs of the corpus. Metrics collected per call included dialog efficiency, dialog quality, task success, and user satisfaction.

*Table 1.*Kinds of action failure

Kinds of action failure		
Potential Cause	**Action Failure**	**Origin / Reason**
Insufficient knowledge about how the task is structured	Inadequate information is provided	User
Inattentive behavior	Erroneous information is provided	User/ excessive cognitive load
Bad signal	Recognition Error	System / noise physical environment
Inadequate lexicon, poor grammar rules or semantic representation frames	Interpretation Error	System/dialog lack of linguistic knowledge
Inadequate management of the discourse state	Contextualization Error	System/poor dialog design

In the following, we will analyze each one of the five potential causes listed in the first column, and we will provide guidelines for preventing their occurrence in practical dialog task. However, before discussing the guidelines we have to introduce some essential notions about the structure of error recovering dialogs.

3.1 The structure of error recovery

As has been illustrated elsewhere in this book, natural language dialog is structured. The structure of two-party dialogs can be analyzed at different levels of granularity. First of all, both human-human and human-machine dialogs are characterized by a *turn-taking* structure; secondly, in a social dialog there are some *conventional segments*, for example at the beginning and at the end of the conversation, such as welcome utterances, greetings, and so on. Third, the part of the dialog occurring between the introduction and the greetings in practical dialogs is usually devoted to the *exchange of information* between conversant for achieving the goal of the conversation. Often this central part of the dialog is structured itself in several different subparts, each one devoted to achieving a subsidiary goal of the conversation. We will refer to those subparts by using the label *subdialogs*. Different kinds of miscommunication may occur in any part of the dialog structure.

As in ordinary human conversation, phenomena such as mishearing and misunderstanding can occur anywhere in the human-machine dialog, but it is important to notice that their occurrence in the conventional segments of a conversation can reduce their disruptive impact due to the more easily predictable semantic content of these segments. For example, if the occurrence of environmental noise prevents the perception of the welcome message of a spoken dialog application, the conversational competence of the user can aid him/her in reconstructing the misperceived parts of the message. On the contrary, mishearing a question can critically affect the prosecution of the dialog since the speaker does not know which information was requested. His/her knowledge of the paralinguistic properties of natural language will allow him/her to process the intonation profile of the utterance. On the basis of this competence, the speaker can infer that the intention of the system was to request some piece of information. Nevertheless, s/he cannot be able to understand the semantic content of the system question. In these cases the user can initiate an error recovery subdialog for obtaining clarifications.

The latter remark introduces us to the problem of clarifying who, in a practical dialog, can initiate an error recovery dialog. The answer is both: both user and system have to able to initiate error recovery routines. Once again, it is important to notice that users can recognize that something is going wrong in the interaction, and s/he can usually detect miscommunication better than system. Thus it is important that spoken dialog system be equipped for being able to recognize users' detection of miscommunication [11]. For implementing this capability the spoken dialog system may exploit knowledge related to the structure of error recovery subdialogs. Actually the subdialogs involving errors have a different structure because they often violate one (or more) general conversational principles. For example, usually speakers interacting with a dialog system reply to system questions by providing the requested information, i.e. they are cooperative and they provide relevant contributions. If that is not the case, the dialog management system should be able to interpret speaker's violation of conversational rules as signals that something was probably going wrong in the previous conversational turns. In next paragraph we will introduce best practice recommendations that may be used for enabling this kind of awareness in practical spoken dialog systems.

4. THE DESIGN OF ERROR RECOVERY SUBDIALOGS

4.1 User-initiated error-recovery subdialogs

While a spoken dialog system can ignore that an error affected the ongoing conversation, users are able to recognize the occurrence of misrecognition or misinterpretation of what they said in previous turns. Most of the potential users of spoken dialog systems recognize that the conversational ability of their artificial partners is limited, and they are usually very explicit in signaling the misunderstanding.

User-initiated repairs usually begin with a turn whose semantic content is not the one expected by the system. For example, if the system was asking a question and the user did not understand the semantic content of that question, s/he can ask to repeat/rephrase the question instead of answering to it.

Any time during the dialog the spoken dialog system has be able to recognize the words and phrasings more frequently uttered for introducing a repair sequence. Of course, these may vary greatly from one natural language to another one, and even sociolinguistic variables can play an important role here. For example, we have noticed that Italians are more direct than Japanese speaking people in correcting the system when it goes wrong.

In the design phase of the dialog strategy, the dialog designer should identify the set of sentences that can introduce user-initiated recovery in the natural language of the application. The best practice recommendation we can offer here is the following

– BPR-1: be aware that users can initiate repair sequences when they do not understand what the system said to him/her
  – For supporting the system in recognizing users' initiation of clarification subdialogs, make your system able to understand the majority of the sentences that can be used to signal misunderstanding in the natural language of the application.

4.2 System-initiated error recovery subdialogs

Sometimes the system may able to understand that misunderstanding occurred. The simplest case occurs when users do not reply to a question asked by the system, i.e. the speech recognition module is not able to perceive the voice signal. These situations are usually labeled as "No Input" in the speech recognition literature. For being able to deal with them at the dialog level, the dialog application designer should provide the opportunity of addressing the user with a sentence that suggests that the user speak aloud or more clearly.

Another common situation occurs when the system understands that the semantic content of the user's sentence is not relevant for continuing the interaction. The following excerpt from a human-machine dialog may clarify this point:

[...]

```
T6   S:   There are too many trains in the morning. Please tell
          me an exact hour between six a.m. and noon.
T7   H:   I do not want to travel with regional trains.
T8   S:   I am sorry, I did not understand. What time do you
          want to leave? Please choose an hour from six to noon.
```

[...]

In turn T6 the system asked the user to provide a precise answer indicating the hour of departure. The user provides such an answer indeed, but it was indirectly formulated. In fact, the user was asking to eliminate from the morning timetable all the regional trains in order to reduce the number of options. However, the dialog system was not able to infer the cooperative user's intention, and the semantic content of turn T7 was considered not relevant for going on in the interaction. In turn T8 the system initiates a repair subdialog by asking again the semantic content of turn T6, and by signaling that it was not able to understand the user's intention. The lack of semantic and pragmatic competence of the system for dealing with indirect speech acts may be annoying, but the system behavior of turn T8 may be useful for suggesting a more explicit interaction style.

A third context where the dialog system can infer a misunderstanding occurs when the system detects that some acquired information is not consistent with other pieces of information already acquired and confirmed by the user. This case is usually originated by an error in the recognition and/or understanding modules of the dialog system. This 'suspect' piece of information should induce the system to initiate a repair subdialog.

The BPR we propose for system-initiated subdialogs is the following:

- BPR-2: Provide your system with appropriate prompts and dialog capabilities for initiating a repair subdialog each time one of the following situations occurs:
  - The user does not provide voice input
  - The user input is not relevant for continuing the dialog
  - The user input is not compatible with previous acquired pieces of information

4.3   Knowledge about how the task is structured

Sometimes ambiguous sentences are consequences of the fact that
speakers are not able to imagine how the dialog task is structured: more
precisely, they do not know which kind of information they have to provide
to the system to solve their problem. Even if users know well the kind of
problem they want to solve by interacting with the system, the dialog
designer should not have to assume that the users know how the system
structures the flow of the information. For example, users of a telephone
train timetable system may not know that for accessing the database of
timetables the system has to know a hypothetic hour of departure: perhaps
they may have been doing that task before with an human travel agent, and
s/he could have guided the dialog in the way around, by asking the desired
time of arrival.

It is thus important to offer anticipations and examples of what the
system will be asking, both at the beginning of the dialog and when one of
the situations analyzed in the previous paragraphs are encountered:BPR-3:
Provide the user with examples of the different kinds of information the
system will ask him. Do this in the introductory message of the application.

To avoid annoying expert users with detailed explanations, offer them the
opportunity of skipping the explanation by uttering a predefined command,
such as "go on", or "skip intro".

4.4   Inattentive user's behavior

Most users are cooperative and they are very careful in answering system
questions or explaining their needs. However, sometimes users provide
inattentive responses. This may happen when users are tired or when the
dialog is not well designed and several, unrelated pieces of information are
requested in the same dialog turn. Dealing explicitly with these factors may
be difficult because the dialog designer should predict the inattentive
behavior of the users in terms of kinds of linguistic errors,
uncooperativeness, and so on. However, the dialog flow may be designed to
reduce the potential disruptions deriving from users' inattentive behavior. In
particular,
– BPR-4: Provide the user with confirmation turns, even if the confidence
   level of the speech recognizer is good; for example, after having acquired
   a set of related semantic values, summarize the acquired information
   before going on in the dialog to give the users the opportunity to correct
   their own mistakes.

4.5 Bad signal and speech recognition errors

Sometimes, especially in telephone dialog applications, the voice signal is very noisy and this causes difficulty for the speech recognizer module. For this reason, when the dialog system detects recognition errors, or when the users signal the occurrence of recognition errors, it is advisable to model the dialog in a way that can help both the user in speaking clearly and help the speech recognition system in focusing on a simpler recognition task. If the speech recognizer used in the application provides the opportunity of taking into account predictions provided by the dialog module, these should be sent in order to focus the language models on the relevant information that will be asked again in the following turn. If repetitive recognition errors occur, it would be advisable to implement a graceful degradation of the recognition modality by passing, for example, from natural language understanding to single word recognition provided that the speech recognition engine is flexible enough to support this shift of recognition modality.

- BPR-5: Provide your voice dialog application with speech recognition objects based on different speech recognition modalities from natural language understanding to recognition of single words.
- BPR-6: When users have difficulties in being understood by the speech recognizer, be able to gradually select more constrained interaction styles.

4.6 Inadequate linguistic knowledge

When the origin of miscommunication is the lack of ability of different system modules in grasping the meaning of users' sentences, this situation is often a signal of poor dialog design. It is important to remember that poor dialog design is not only a matter of coverage of the speech recognition grammars or poor training of the language models, but it may also be originated by inadequate system prompts.

The way information is asked greatly influences the way users formulate their replies. Several human factors studies demonstrate a tendency of the users to imitate the interaction style of their conversational partners. In particular, it is important to design system prompts that are compatible with the recognition capabilities that will be selected in any dialog turn. For example, it would not be advisable to ask a very general question in a dialog turn when the active speech recognition grammar is able to grasp just few information items.

Spoken dialog applications devoted to the general public are very problematic in this respect because multiple users could use the system from time to time, and these potential users may have very different age, education, and familiarity with automatic systems. Novice users of spoken dialog systems usually prefer to be guided in the dialog, while expert users would prefer to guide the interaction by themselves. It is important to find a balance between these two requirements, but our suggestion is to prioritize the requirements of the novice users. That can be done by formulating very clear system prompts, by avoiding vague questions, and by reinforcing the speech recognition grammars with the ability to deal with some more complex sentences that the expert users could utter [12]. Of course, speech recognition grammar or language models should be powerful enough to cover most frequent user formulations, but this issue is dealt with in a different chapter of the present book [13]. Here we just recommend that the work of designing speech recognition grammars and the one of designing the prompts of the system be joint activities because the effect of prompts on users' linguistic behavior is very valuable.

Thus the best practice recommendations for preventing errors due to inadequate system knowledge are:

– BPR-7: Provide your system with speech recognition grammar and/or language models able to cover the most frequent users' sentences in any turn of the dialog;

– BPR-8: Design the system prompts by taking into account the linguistic behavior you would like to obtain by the user, and by taking into account the capabilities of the speech recognition engine in any particular turn of the dialog.

The issue of adequacy of system prompts is very relevant and it is addressed in the next paragraph too.

4.7   Repetitive errors due to inadequate system prompts

Since repetitive recognition or dialog errors are perhaps the main source of frustration a user can experience when interacting with a spoken dialog system, we would like to discuss an example illustrating how their impact could be reduced.

Most of repetitive errors are due to recognition problems. They often occur when the system vocabulary contains a huge quantity of words belonging to the same lexical category, for example personal proper names in automatic directory assistance services, or geographical proper names in vocal car navigation systems.

In the previous paragraph, we said that a careful design of the interaction between speech recognition and dialog capabilities can help in reducing the annoying impact of these errors in the dialog. Let us consider the following dialog excerpt[3]:

```
T1    S:   Automatic Railway Information System.Please, remember
           to speak after the tone. How may I help you?
T2    H:   Oh yes: (.) I'd like to know if there is a train (.)
           leaving on Saturday (.) leaving from Torino, going to
           Milan.
T3    S:   Leaving from Torino, going to Milano.Is that correct?
           Please answer yes or no.
T4    H:   Yes:
T5    S:   Would you like to leave eight am? Please answer yes or
           no.
T6:   H:   No:
T5    S:   What time would you like to leave? Please give a
           one-word answer only.
T7    H:   Eight in the evening.
T8    S:   I am sorry, I did not understand. What time do you
           want to leave? Please give a one-word answer only.
T9    H:   Eight
T10   S:   Departing time: eight am. Is that correct? Please
           answer yes or no.
T11   H:   No
T12   S:   Please, repeat what time do you want to leave.
T13   H:   Eight
T14   S:   Departing time: eight am. Is that correct? Please
           answer yes or no.
T15   H:   No
```

The dialog above is an example of repetitive errors that are due to inadequacies of dialog design. The welcome message of the system is formulated for inviting the users to adopt a conversational interaction style, but at this stage of the dialog the system is only able to consider two information elements, departure and arrival. The system can only accept the words "yes" or "no" when a confirmation is required (T3). Actually, after obtaining the confirmation of departure and arrival, the system prompts the user for getting the confirmation of the time information. The time provided by the user is ambiguous because he did not add the specification 'am' or

---

[3] The dialog is taken from a corpus collected in March-April 1993, at the CSELT (*Centro Studi E Laboratori Telecomunicazioni*) lab in Torino, Italy. The interaction language was Italian; for simplicity, the original Italian text has been omitted, the translation is by the author. In the transcription the symbol "(.)" stands for a pause, while the symbol ":" stands for a hesitation resulting in a longer last sound of the word (notice that in Italian this is almost always a vowel).

'pm'. The system interprets 'eight' as 'eight am', while the user intended 'eight pm'. User's turn T7 disambiguates the user's intention, but at this stage of the dialog the system entered a recovery strategy based on isolated word recognition; as a consequence, the specification was not understood by the dialog system.

4.8   Inadequate management of the discourse state

Contextualization errors are another important cause of miscommunication between humans and machines. Several problems in human-machine communication originate from the fact that the user's focus and the system's focus are not aligned: the consequence of this discrepancy is that user may want to provide information that the system is not able to understand or deal with in that particular state of the discourse. For avoiding this difficulty it would be important to give the user a coherent idea of the understanding capabilities of the system. In fact, on the one hand the user is conscious of the limited semantic competence of the system, but s/he might not be aware of the fact that the dialog application constrains the interpretation focus. Actually, when the dialog system or the user initiates an error recovery subdialog, the focus of the interaction is usually restricted to the information that was not understood. This focus restriction is useful because it may be accompanied by analogous restrictions of speech recognition grammar and/or vocabulary. During the evaluation of spoken dialog interfaces devoted to large populations of potential users, we have often observed that when users correct some errors they are not interested in providing information other than the correction. However, the users need to know that the system is checking some pieces of the information they entered, and also that something probably went wrong in some previous turns of the dialog. Respecting the following Best Practice Recommendations could decrease the impact of this problem:
–   BPR-9: When the system initiates a repair subdialog, the user needs to be aware that the dialog system is trying to correct some pieces of information that were erroneously acquired. The system prompts have to be designed to communicate the discourse state to the user.
–   BPR-10: If your error recovery design requires a graceful degradation of the recognition capabilities (for example, passing from continuous speech understanding to isolated word recognition) make sure that the user can understand that s/he is expected to utter simple phrases or single words.

5. HOW USERS SIGNAL MISUNDERSTANDING

One of the problems of error recovery is to enable the dialog system to recognize users' corrections. This task is straightforward if users' sentences contain explicit remarks about misunderstanding, such as "No", "It's wrong", and so on. However, users' linguistic behavior may not contain any explicit negation word. Special attention should be paid to repetitions.

In human-machine dialog repetitions with function of correction are very frequent, partly because of the errors of the vocal recognizer [15].

Repetition also contributes to the process of comprehension. In the dialog between human beings this process is gradual, while in human-machine dialogs we cannot speak of gradualness. The automatic system either understands or not in relation to each piece of task relevant information.

During a conversation humans resort to inferential mechanisms, and also to world knowledge, while the system knowledge is limited to the task specific domain. Therefore while in human-human conversations, what is explicitly said and what is just implied have both meaning, in the dialog with an automatic dialog system everything has to be made explicit.

In some cases, the misunderstanding that causes repetition is due to the non-mutuality of beliefs between the user and the system. Total or partial repetition helps when the user makes a mistake or the speech recognize does not recognize exactly.

6. CONCLUSIONS

In this chapter we have claimed that designing effective error recovery strategies is important for increasing usability of practical dialog applications. We have discussed ten best practice recommendations for designing error recovery subdialogs in practical spoken dialog applications: they are summarized in Table 2.

Dealing with misunderstanding is one of the most challenging design issues in human-machine interaction: there is no privileged theory which predicts how a speaker can behave under error conditions, any more than there is a "true" scientific account of *creativity*. However we can increase the usability of our practical dialog systems if we take into account that misperception, misrecognition, and misunderstanding are constitutive modes of oral human-machine discourse, and that common knowledge about the discourse state can help to reduce their disruptive impact on the quality of communication.

Table 2. Ten best practices for designing error recovery dialogs

BPR	Focusing on	How to do this, i.e., provide your dialog system with the following abilities
1	User-initiated repair	Understanding typical repair phrases
2	System-initiated repair	Dealing with user's silence, repetitions or corrections
3	Providing examples	Examples of key commands that are always active
4	Confirmation turns	Initiating confirmation sequences
5	Adaptation of recognizer capabilities to the discourse state	On-line selection of different speech recognition objects
6	Graceful degradation of the degree of initiative	Passing smoothly through different recognition modalities depending on the discourse state
7	Tuning of speech understanding module	Good coverage of frequently used idioms, domain dependent phrases, opening and closing sequences, etc...
8	Eliciting "fair" linguistic behavior	Adapting prompts for eliciting simple and concise users' utterances
9	Facilitating the user's recognition of the discourse state	Communicating to the user that the system is entering a repair subdialog
10	Increasing user's awareness of system capabilities	Communicating that the system expects a more concise linguistic behavior

REFERENCES

[1] S. W. McRoy, "Detecting, Repairing and Preventing Human-Machine Miscommunication," in Working Notes of the AAAI-96 Workshop at the Thirteenth National Conference on Artificial Intelligence, 1996.

[2] J. L. Austin, How to Do Things with Words. Cambridge, Mass.: Harvard University Press, 1962.

[3] H. P. Grice, "Logic and conversation," in Syntax and semantics, vol. 3, P. Cole and J. Morgan, Eds. New York: Academic Press, 1975, pp. 41-58.

[4] J. R. Searle, Speech acts: An essay in the philosophy of language. London: Cambridge University Press, 1969.

[5] S. C. Levinson, Pragmatics. Cambridge, England: Cambridge University Press, 1983.

[6] J. S. Bruner, "The ontogenesis of speech acts," Journal of Child Language, vol. 2, pp. 1-19.

[7] T. Winograd, "What does it mean to understand language?," Cognitive Science, vol. 4, pp. 209--241, 1980.

[8] J. F. Allen and R. Perrault, "Analyzing intention in utterances," Artificial Intelligence, vol. 15, pp. 143--178, 1980.

[9] R. Ardito, B. Bara, and E. Blanzieri, "A cognitive account of situated communication," Psychological Science, in press.

[10]   D. Traum and Dillenbourg, "Miscommunication in Multi-Modal Collaboration," presented at Working Notes of the AAAI-96 Workshop at the Thirteenth National Conference on Artificial Intelligence, Portland, Oregon, USA, 1996.

[11]   M. Danieli, "On the use of expectations for detecting and repairing human-machine miscommunication," presented at Detecting, Repairing, and Preventing Human-Machine Miscommunications: Working Notes of the AAAI-96 Workshop at the Thirteenth National Conference on Artificial Intelligence, Portland, Oregon, USA, 1996.

[12]   J. A. Larson, "Voice User Interface Design for Novice and Experienced Users," This volume.

[13]   K. Godden, "How to Wreck a Nice Speech Grammar," This volume.

Chapter 5

Visualization Tools for Designing Spoken Dialogs

Deborah A. Dahl
Conversational Technologies

Key words: speech application development tools, spoken dialog design, visualization

Abstract: Designing sophisticated spoken human-computer dialogs is difficult both because dialogs can become extremely complex and also because spoken dialogs by definition are auditory, not visual. Therefore there is no obvious mapping of a spoken dialog design to a visual representation that can be used in a design tool. Nevertheless, tools for dialog design are very important, and there have been many attempts to develop useful tools to aid developers in designing spoken dialogs. This paper discusses a number of approaches to dialog visualization and points out considerations that need to be taken into account when selecting a tool for a particular project.

1.   PROBLEM

Spoken human-computer dialogs are difficult to design for many reasons. For example, there are many gaps in our understanding of the human factors of how people interact with speech interfaces. This problem has been the focus of considerable research. In addition, there is a great deal of practical knowledge in this area gained from the analysis of deployed applications (see, for example, the papers in [1]). This paper focuses on a second problem that has received much less attention. That is, how can a developer who is focused on the details of scripting a complex dialog, develop an understanding of the entire dialog, making sure that all paths through the dialog are reasonable and consistent, and that the dialog as a whole doesn't contain dead ends or loops? Mixed initiative and user initiative dialogs in particular have many complexities introduced by the freedom of the user to change the direction of the dialog at any time. When all of these situations have to be individually anticipated by the designer, the complexities can become overwhelming. It's easy to assume that graphical dialog design tools will automatically provide a solution to this problem, but tools that aren't a good fit to the design task can do more harm than good.

There are many design tools available in the speech industry now. These tools adopt different approaches to assisting designers in their tasks. How can we know what's the best dialog design tool for a specific project? This paper looks at a number of approaches to dialog design tools, points out advantages and disadvantages of each approach and provides some dimensions for classifying tools.

Although there are many types of spoken human-computer dialogs, the focus in this paper is on designs for the form-filling tasks and navigational dialogs that are by far the most commonly encountered types of dialogs in commercial systems. By form-filling dialogs, we mean dialogs where the task centers on obtaining several pieces of information from a user and then acting on that information. Travel reservations, finding a certain type of restaurant, and placing orders are good examples of form-filling dialogs. An example of a navigational dialog is the kind of dialog that might be encountered in a voice portal where the user is asked questions that allow the system to navigate to a particular application. Other types of dialogs potentially will require quite different dialog design tools. In the future these other types of dialogs may be more frequently deployed, and may require different thinking about tools for dialog design.

Another type of dialog which this paper does not address is multimodal dialogs, which contain visual components as well as spoken ones. Due to the presence of the graphical interface, graphical tools for designing multimodal dialogs will be very different from tools for designing voice-only dialogs.

2. VISUALIZING DIALOGS

One important component of most design is visualization, or how a non-visual concept or data can be displayed visually in a meaningful and conceptually transparent way. The main point of this paper is to compare different approaches to visualization in designing dialogs, but it will also discuss other general considerations in tool selection.

The appropriate type of visualization for a particular task depends on how the underlying task is conceptually structured. There is considerable research literature on visualization for various kinds of abstract data, for example, the papers in [2]. However, very little work has directly focused on effective visualizations for spoken human- omputer dialogs. Visualization is an especially interesting problem for voice-only spoken dialogs because they don't have an obvious visual component. Consequently, the relationship between the dialog design and its visual representation is more abstract than in other design tasks.

Although many tools which are intended to help application developers design dialogs are currently commercially available, this paper won't discuss specific tools. Because the tool marketplace evolves very rapidly, any discussion of specific tools would quickly become out of date. For that reason, it will be much more useful to focus here on generic approaches. In some cases the generic approaches discussed have been realized in an existing tool, but in other cases they have not. Keeping the discussion at a generic level will make it possible to use some of the considerations discussed in this paper to evaluate and select future tools as well as those currently available. For those who are interested in current products, some references to web resources for finding current tools are provided at the end of this paper.

3. THE ROLE OF TOOLS IN DEVELOPMENT

In current dialog design tools, there are several different philosophies as to what the designer's task is, leading to very different graphical interfaces. One important contrast is between tools for designing dialogs and tools for supporting a native dialog scripting language.[1] One example of a native dialog scripting language is VoiceXML [3]. VoiceXML is based on XML (eXtensible Markup Language [4]), and is executed by an engine called a voice browser. VoiceXML is being standardized by the World Wide Web Consortium and it integrates voice applications with the Web. Because of the popularity of VoiceXML, and the fact that it is an open standard, we will use it as an example of a native dialog scripting language in this paper. However, the points discussed in this paper would also apply to other dialog scripting languages.

Many graphical tools have been developed to assist in the task of creating VoiceXML markup. While the goal of these tools is ultimately to end up with a good dialog design, this goal is accomplished indirectly by assisting the designer in creating VoiceXML. Because of this indirection, the

---

[1] A scripting language allows a developer to specify a script for a dialog that will be executed at runtime by a dialog management engine. It is also possible to develop dialogs using standard programming languages. Most of what we say about dialogs that use scripting languages also applies to dialogs that are implemented directly with programming languages.

developer has to focus on how to express the dialog in VoiceXML terms, such as forms, menus and fields, rather than more generic dialog concepts.

In contrast, another approach to dialog design tools is to consider the goal of the tool to be that of assisting the developer in the task of designing a dialog. From that perspective, the specific native format, for example, VoiceXML, is greatly deemphasized. The primitives in the tool will be basic dialog concepts, such as prompts and turns, abstracted away from the details of the scripting language. One claim of this paper is that the more directly the tool maps to generic dialog concepts the easier it will be to use and the better the resulting dialogs will be.

Finally, we discuss a very high level approach to dialog design that involves designing a *task*, rather than a dialog per se. This means that the developer specifies *what* is to be accomplished, and the details of *how* it is to be accomplished in a specific dialog are left up to the dialog management software that is executing the design.

4.   EXAMPLE DIALOG

In order to compare various approaches to visualizing dialogs, we will consider one sample spoken dialog and show how the same dialog can be represented with different tools. In order to keep the examples clear, they will be significantly simplified from the functionality that would be required by a real application. For example, there are no events, no scripting, and no error handling, all of which would add to the complexity of the exposition, and yet are always needed in any real application.

The sample application is an air travel reservation system with three stages (1) identifying the user (2) getting the
flight details, and (3) confirming the itinerary.

Here's an example of the kind of dialog that this application would support:

1. System: Welcome to the flight information system. Please state your userid and pin.
2. User: My user id is 12345 and my pin is 1111.
3. System: Please state the city you will be flying from, the city you will be flying to, and your departure date and time.
4. User: I'm going from Philadelphia to Boston.
5. System: On what date do you want to depart?
6. User: On January 10 and I want to leave around 10:00 a.m.

7. System: You have inquired about flights from Philadelphia to Boston
             on January 10 leaving at 10:00 a.m. Is this correct?
8. User: Yes.

Figure 1. Example travel dialog

Note that this application supports mixed initiative, where the user can supply information that wasn't directly requested by the system, as in utterance 6. The application also allows the user to supply less information than was requested, as in utterance 4. It then follows up with system directed utterances to collect the missing information, as in utterance 5.

4.1   Native Scripting Formats

We start with the baseline case of developing a dialog without tools other than a text editor or generic programming language IDE. Most dialog management systems support dialog design using a native scripting language. A good example of this is VoiceXML. VoiceXML dialogs can be developed using any text editor. Advantages of using simple tools for developing a dialog script include the availability of the full power of the scripting language and lower cost. Furthermore, there's no need to train developers to use a particular tool and the project isn't dependent on a specific tool vendor. The disadvantages include a longer development and test time and a greater chance of introducing errors and inconsistencies.

This type of design flexibility is well supported by the VoiceXML Form Interpretation Algorithm (FIA), which specifies the procedural execution process for the declarative VoiceXML markup.

Here's the VoiceXML markup that underlies the dialog in *Figure 1.*

```
<?xml version="1.0" encoding="UTF-8"?>
<vxml version="2.0">
  <var name="userid"/>
  <var name="pin"/>
  <form id="welcome">
    <initial>
      <prompt>Welcome to the flight information system.
Please state your user id and pin.</prompt>
    </initial>
    <grammar src="welcome.grxml"/>
    <field modal="true" name="userid" type="digits">
      <prompt>Please state your 5 digit userid.</prompt>
    </field>
    <field modal="true" name="pin" type="digits">
      <prompt>Please state your 4 digit pin.</prompt>
    </field>
```

```
    <filled>
      <goto next="#get_details"/>
    </filled>
  </form>
  <form id="get_details">
    <initial>
      <prompt>Please state the city you will be flying
from, the city you will be flying to, and your departure
date and time.</prompt>
    </initial>
    <grammar src="details.grm"/>
    <field modal="true" name="from_city">
      <prompt>Where will you be flying from?</prompt>
      <grammar src="cities.grxml"/>
    </field>
    <field modal="true" name="to_city">
      <prompt>Where will you be flying to?</prompt>
      <grammar src="cities.grxml"/>
    </field>
    <field modal="true" name="departure_date"
type="date">
      <prompt>On what date would you like to
depart?</prompt>
    </field>
    <field modal="true" name="departure_time"
type="time">
      <prompt>At what time would you like to
depart?</prompt>
    </field>
    <field name="confirm_details" type="boolean">
      <prompt>You have inquired about flights from<value
expr="from_city"/>to <value expr="to_city"/>on<value
expr="departure_date"/>at<value expr="departure_time."/>
        <break msecs="300"/>is this correct?</prompt>
      <filled>
        <if cond="confirm_details">
          <else/>
          <clear namelist="to_city from_city
departure_date departure_time"/>
        </if>
        <submit namelist="to_city from_city
departure_date departure_time userid pin"
next="http://airline_server.com/reservation"/>
      </filled>
    </field>
  </form>
</vxml>
```

Figure 2. VoiceXML markup for an airline reservation application

Clearly, it is very difficult to understand the overall dialog design from the VoiceXML markup shown in *Figure 2*. For example, because XML syntax doesn't differentiate among elements on the basis of their semantics, the <form> tag, which encloses an entire dialog, doesn't look visually distinct from the <break> tag, which has the much lower level function of introducing a break into utterances that will be rendered using text-to-speech. In addition, the high level structure of the dialog is difficult to understand in the native format. Following the callflow requires knowledge of the VoiceXML FIA, and the path of <goto> elements. While this markup is complex already, the complexity would be dramatically increased if the sample dialog were not unrealistically simple. So there is a real benefit to looking at alternative ways of representing this dialog which reveal more of its organization and structure.

4.2 Tools for Improving the Process of Developing Native Scripting Formats

4.2.1 Tree-Based VoiceXML Representations

For VoiceXML dialogs, or any XML-based scripting language, one approach is to display a tree representing the XML tree structure of the VoiceXML document. We can classify tree-based representations into two types, standard XML tools, and VoiceXML-aware tools. There are many standard tools available for editing general XML documents, and these can be used for editing VoiceXML documents as well, for example XMLSpy [5]. The advantage of these generic tools is that there are very many of them as opposed to the number of tools that are available specifically for VoiceXML. The disadvantage is that they can't take into account any VoiceXML specifics, other than those defined by the syntax of the language. Because they don't have any specific information about VoiceXML, it's not possible to represent different components of VoiceXML differently. A tree representation of this kind can be seen in *Figure 3*.

4.2.1.1 Semantic Highlighting.
In contrast, a Voice-XML-aware tool can take the specifics of VoiceXML into account. Typically these tools have a palette of VoiceXML elements that can be inserted into the tree structure. For any selected point in the tree, only XML elements and attributes that are valid according to the definition of the VoiceXML language (in terms of the DTD or XML Schema) are available. This is useful for developers who may not be completely familiar with VoiceXML syntax, and is very helpful for learning.

We can see the contrast between these approaches by comparing *Figure 3* with *Figure 4*.

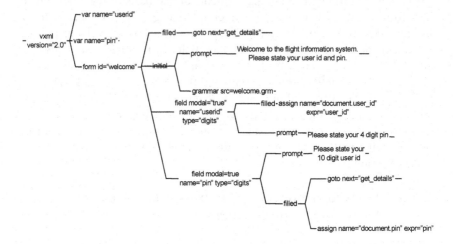

Figure 3. XML tree for the first form of the airline reservation application

Figure 3 shows a generic XML tree representation for the airline example shown in *Figure 1*. All of the tags have equal status because the tool has no way of knowing about the semantics of the various tags; that is the specific functions of each tag and it relative importance. Although the representation is clearer than *Figure 2*, we can't see the relative importance or function of the tags by looking at the representation.

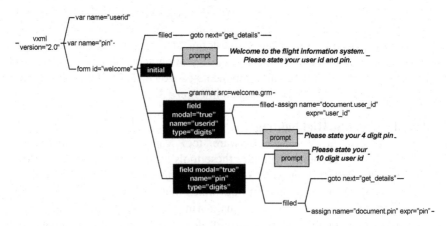

Figure 4. VoiceXML-aware XML tree representation for the first form of the airline reservation application

Figure 4, on the other hand, shows how a VoiceXML-aware tool could distinguish tags with different semantic functions. If the tool is aware of the VoiceXML concept of a "field item",[2] for example, it can distinctively highlight the field items ("initial" and "field" in this dialog). The field items in *Figure 4* are highlighted in black. Similarly, as the figure shows, the tool could also informatively highlight branches of other tags, such as prompts, highlighted in gray here. This provides an improvement in clarity because the developer is able to immediately identify tags of specific types.

4.2.1.2 Focusing on specific areas of the design.

As dialogs become more complex, it's helpful for the developer to have techniques for focusing on specific areas of the design. Here we describe two such techniques, collapsing branches and zooming.

Collapsing branches

A very useful feature of most XML editing tools is that the developer has the ability to expand and collapse tree branches. This is very useful for complex applications, because it allows the developer to focus on the details of the part of the dialog that's being worked on, without being distracted by complexities of the rest of the dialog. This can be seen in *Figure 5*, where parts of the dialog have been collapsed so that the developer can focus on the "confirm_details" field. Branches that have been collapsed are shown in gray.

---

[2] A field item in VoiceXML represents a dialog unit that collects one piece of information.

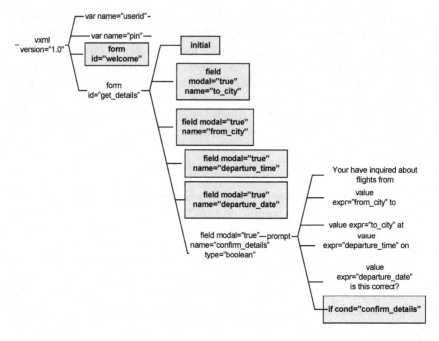

Figure 5. XML tree with collapsed branches

Zooming

With a tree display, it's important to keep the branches of the tree from taking up too much space, because it's very important for the developer to be able to see as much of the relevant portion of the dialog in one screen as possible. Scrolling, especially horizontal scrolling, is a major distraction. Because VoiceXML (or any XML-based markup) is very verbose, it's easy for a relatively short dialog to take up a lot of space in a design tool.   In addition, some of the tags, for example, the <var> declaration, don't have much content, yet they take up a whole branch of the XML tree. So it's very important to keep the display of the branches compact. Zooming capabilities allow the designer to focus closely on portions of the design that are of immediate interest, and to zoom out to look at the dialog at a high level, with less detail.

Insuring dialog consistency with focusing strategies

Unfortunately, the tactic of focusing on specific areas of the dialog and ignoring others can lead to global consistency problems. Although there's no simple answer to this problem, it can be alleviated in several ways:

1. give developers best practice guidelines
2. build in common capabilities (for example, asking for help)
3. use reusable components

4. design a clear and consistent persona for the computer prompts (for example making sure that the persona conveyed by the prompts doesn't appear to be formal and businesslike in one prompt but casual and informal in the next),
5. make sure that the dialog is reviewed for consistency at multiple points.

However, there's no ideal solution, and some combination of these suggestions is probably the best way to insure the consistency of dialogs.

4.2.1.3 Other tool utilities.
Cut and paste

Another useful feature of tree-based tools is that cutting and pasting of tree branches is also generally supported. It's important to have this capability, but it's usually a little more cumbersome to use than the parallel task of cutting and pasting of arbitrary text in a text editor. There are a couple of reasons for this. First, cutting and pasting has to be done on whole branches, while any text can be cut from a text document whether it's a well-formed tree branch or not. In addition, with a GUI tree-based tool, it can take several steps to identify where the material is to be pasted.

Editing native markup

Often tools also allow the developer to view and/or edit the native script markup by switching to another view. This seems useful, but should be viewed with caution. The ability to edit the native markup directly may be a sign that the tool doesn't fully support all the scripting language's features. That is, in principle, it shouldn't be necessary to edit the native markup if the tool fully supports the scripting language. Editing native markup in the context of a tool is also problematic because the syntax may not be checked until the editing is complete and the developer attempts to return to the GUI interface. At that point, if there's a syntax error, the syntax checker will prevent the developer from returning to the GUI screen. This may leave the developer with the task of figuring out what piece of the newly added markup caused the problem and possibly redoing a lot of work.

4.2.2 Nested Boxes

For VoiceXML, or other XML-based scripting languages, a variation on the tree approach is to represent the XML tree by collapsible nested boxes as opposed to an explicit tree, with each box corresponding to a branch of the tree. There isn't much practical difference between these visualizations. Boxes are useful because indicating that a box is selected can be done by coloring the box, which is visually very distinctive. On the other hand, boxes take up more space than trees and the hierarchical dialog structure is less apparent. *Figure 6* shows the airline reservation application as represented with nested boxes.

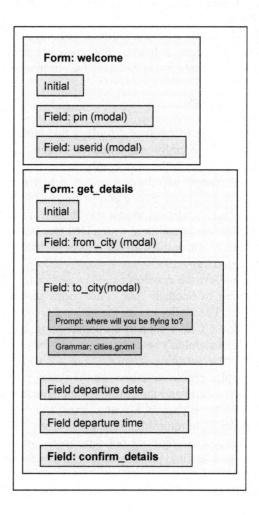

Figure 6. XML tree represented as nested boxes

4.3   Tools for Designing Dialogs

The discussion above had to do with tools for making the process of developing a dialog in a native scripting language, using VoiceXML as an example, easier and more intuitive. To use the tools described above, it's necessary to know the native language fairly well, although the tools can help with some of the details. On the other hand, if we agree that the ultimate goal of the developer is to create a dialog, then creating the script document is just a means to that end. By focusing on a script document, for example a VoiceXML document, the developer is required to think at the level of "should there be a <form> or a <menu> here?", "what are the conditions for entering this field", and "what should I call this variable?" These are questions about VoiceXML, not about the dialog. The dialog designer should be thinking about higher level questions such as "what choices does the user have at this point?", "when should help be offered?" Going from authoring in a scripting language like VoiceXML to designing a dialog requires a conceptual shift. Besides allowing the designer to focus on the dialog rather than the scripting language, benefits of using a dialog visualization include the following:

– Because the tool requires less familiarity with the scripting language, design work can more easily be done by dialog designers as opposed to programmers, which will result in a better dialog design
– Because the design is abstracted from the runtime scripting language that is used to implement it, it's not necessary to commit to a target scripting language during development. The runtime script can be automatically generated by a tool when it is needed in a particular implementation. This feature might be used, for example, if the application is intended to run in both VoiceXML and SALT [6] environments.

4.4   Visualizing dialogs

We can look at several approaches to tools for dialog design. We will first be concerned with dialogs that are based on a series of well-defined states where the dialog flow moves deterministically from one state to another. We will discuss two related approaches to visualizing state-based dialogs (1) networks or graphs and (2) flowcharts.

4.4.1 Networks

One approach that seems very natural is to represent the dialog as a directed graph of states and transitions or network. Each state corresponds to a more or less self-contained portion of the overall dialog. Transitions are the various conditions that cause a dialog to move from one state to another. A network representation of the airline dialog can be seen in *Figure 7*. The key point about this representation to note is that the nodes represent states of the dialog, as opposed to scripting language constructs. On the one hand

98   *Deborah Dahl*

this gives the developer a more abstract view of the dialog, but on the other
hand, it hides the details of the scripting language, so that it may be hard for
the developer to understand what's going on at a low level of the dialog.
This visualization may also include arrows on the transitions indicating the
temporal flow between states. This is appealing for a simple dialog, but can
easily become too complex if the dialog contains many states and transitions.

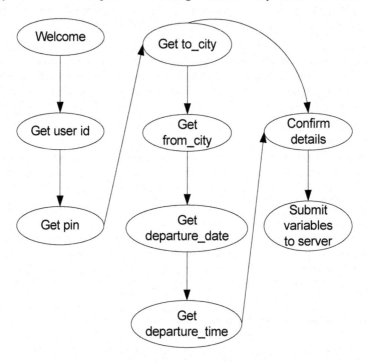

Figure 7. Network representation of a dialog

4.4.2 Flowcharts

A variation on the network representation that adds more detail on
transitions is a flowchart, as seen in *Figure 8*. This flowchart is functionally
identical to the network in *Figure 7*, with the addition of transition
information. For example, from this flowchart we can see that the dialog can
go directly from the welcome state to the "get_details" state if the userid and
pin are known; that is, if they were spoken in the first response to the
"welcome" prompt.

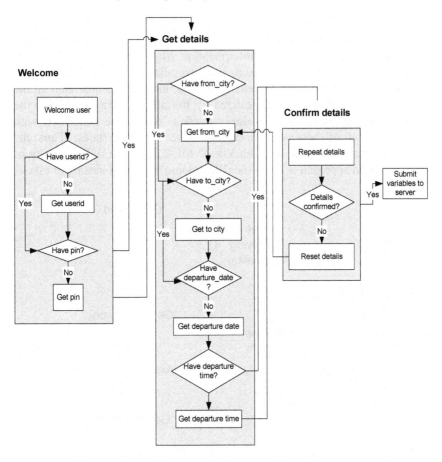

Figure 8. Flowchart representation of a dialog

4.4.3 Task-based Visualization

The most abstract approach we will discuss here is task-based. The approaches that we've discussed so far have been largely state-based, where the dialog is conceptualised as a series of more or less self-contained states. The task-based approach is not a representation of a dialog as much as it's a representation of a task that will be accomplished through a dialog. A task-based representation is a hierarchically-structured representation which starts from an overall high level task, such as making an airline reservation, and breaks it into subtasks which have to be performed in order to complete the overall task. The actual dialog results from the dialog manager's execution of the task description. There are no explicit dialog states in this model.

VoiceXML itself has elements of this approach. A VoiceXML form can be thought of as a representation of a task, with fields as subtasks. Because VoiceXML relies on the Form Interpretation Algorithm to render the form temporally, quite complex mixed initiative dialogs can be represented relatively easily by a series of fields in a form, in effect summarizing all the possible dialogs that could be realized by the different ways in which the fields could be filled. The developer doesn't have to be concerned with representing all of these possible dialogs as sequences of states. Thus, the most important difference between VoiceXML 2.0 and the full generality of the task-based approach is that VoiceXML doesn't support nesting of tasks.

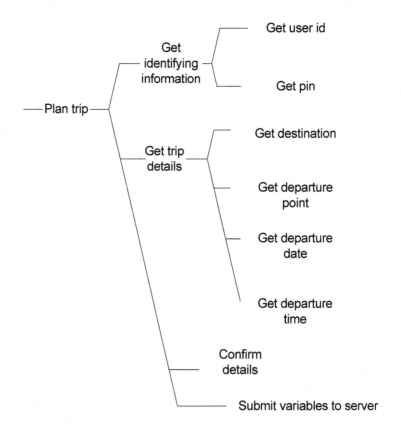

Figure 9. Task-based dialog representation

Figure 9 shows the airline reservation application as a hierarchically-structured list of tasks that have to be accomplished in order to complete the overall task of making an airline reservation. Although it is tree-structured, it's important to note that this example differs from the tree and box representations discussed in Section 4.2.1and Section 4.2.2 because it's a way of visualizing the task to be performed, not a way of visualizing the underlying scripting language. This approach naturally lends itself to representing mixed initiative dialogs, because it doesn't make a commitment to the exact order in which these tasks have to be performed.[3] However, this very abstraction means that the design may be hard to debug, since during debugging is exactly when the developer needs to see the low level details.

4.5 Summary of tools discussion

Table 2 summarizes the advantages and disadvantages of the various approaches to visualizing dialogs discussed in this paper.

Although today's tools are very focused on specific representations, the ideal future tool would combine the advantages of different representations. It would have the ability to visualize the design at multiple levels, including the high-level abstract task representation, the tree-based representation of the native script, all the way down to the actual native format itself.

---

[3] Because of this high-level view, the task-based approach also lends itself to device-independence. That is, the information described by a task representation could potentially be presented (1) as part of a spoken dialog, (2) as part of a graphical dialog (3) specialized for devices with differing graphical capabilities, or (4) it could be presented as part of a multimodal interface.

Table 2. Summary of tool approaches

Tool Represents	Visual Representation	Advantages	Disadvantages
Scripting language	Text	Simplicity Low cost Familiarity Vendor-independent	Hard to understand Error prone
	Generic XML tree	Many generic tools	Doesn't represent dialog semantics
	Specific XML tree	Can represent dialog semantics	Fewer tools available
Dialog	Nested boxes	Color coding possible	Boxes take up space Hard to compare levels of nesting in different boxes
	Graph/network	View dialog Clear for simple dialogs	Don't see transitional conditions Hard to follow if complex
	Flowchart	View dialog Clear for simple dialogs	Hard to follow if complex
Task	Tree	Easy to understand global dialog structure	High level view obscures details

5. GENERAL ISSUES AND SELECTION CRITERIA

So far in this paper we've examined only one aspect of dialog development tools — the support they give authors for designing and visualizing dialogs. However, in practice, many other criteria for selecting tools are important as well.

While a good dialog visualization strategy is an important aspect of the utility of a tool, it's only one aspect of what needs to be taken into account in selecting a tool for a real project. Many other considerations have to be taken into account in making a selection, and sometimes practical considerations such as the platforms where the tool runs, the languages that it supports, and its cost, have to take priority over factors that make the tool easy to use to design effective dialogs. Consequently, it's important to understand what the alternatives and tradeoffs are when a decision has to be made.

5.1 Tool Selection Criteria

Every project has its own requirements, and selection of a tool for a specific project will ultimately depend on how that tool meets the requirements of that project. In this section we briefly list some of the other important evaluation criteria for tools.

1. Does the project have a requirement for specific languages? Clearly the tool must support development in the languages required by the project.
2. If a project either has many complex dialog states, or includes a lot of natural language understanding with its associated complex grammars, then it will be more important to use a GUI-based tool, because otherwise the complexity of the dialog can become overwhelming.
3. Some tools require proprietary runtime components to run the dialogs generated by the tool. Being able to avoid commitments to a proprietary runtime environment may or may not be important to a particular project, but this needs to be considered.
4. Vendor stability and commitment to support for a tool during the project's lifetime are important aspects of any selection process for third party software.
5. The need for full support in the tool for the capabilities of the native scripting language should be considered.
6. Tools also vary in their degree of support for many other aspects of the development of spoken dialog systems in addition to dialog design. For example, it's very convenient to have graphical tools for grammar development, for simulation and testing, and for prompt development. For any particular project these may become very important.

6.   CONCLUSION

This paper has examined many approaches to visualizing dialog designs and discussed the pros and cons of each approach. With this information, it is hoped that developers of spoken dialog projects will be able to select the best available tools to use to design the best possible dialog for their application — user-friendly, robust, effective and maintainable. This is a very dynamic area and for that reason it's difficult to give pointers to specific tools without the information quickly becoming out of date. However, readers who are interested in finding out about currently available tools should look for information presented at conferences and trade shows such as SpeechTEK and the Applied Voice Input Output Society (AVIOS). Websites such as [7, 8] also provide information about currently available products.

7.   ACKNOWLEDGEMENTS

Many of the ideas described here on task-based approaches were originally developed in discussions with Lewis Norton and Marcia Linebarger. I am also grateful to the World Wide Web Consortium's Voice Browser Working Group for many discussions about VoiceXML and human-computer dialogs in general. I also received very helpful comments on an earlier version of this paper from Patti Price.

REFERENCES

[1] D. Gardner-Bonneau, *Human Factors and Voice Interactive Systems*. Boston: Kluwer Academic Publishers, 1999.

[2] S. K. Card, J. D. Mackinlay, and B. Shneiderman, *Readings in Information Visualization: Using Vision to Think*. San Francisco, California: Morgan Kaufmann, 1999.

[3] W3C, "Voice Extensible Markup Language (VoiceXML 2.0) http://www.w3.org/TR/voicexml20/", http://www.w3.org/TR/voicexml20/, 2002.

[4] W3C, "Extensible Markup Language (XML) 1.0 (Second Edition)", http://www.w3.org/TR/REC-xml, 2000.

[5] "ALTOVA - XML development, data mapping, and content authoring tools", http://www.xmlspy.com,

[6] "Salt Forum", http://www.saltforum.org, 2002.

[7] K. Rehor, "VoiceXML Development Tools", http://www.kenrehor.com/voicexml/#tools, 2003.

[8] palowireless, "VoiceXML Development Tools", http://www.palowireless.com/voicexml/devtools.asp,

Chapter 6

How to Wreck a Nice Speech Grammar

Kurt Godden
General Motors R&D

Key words: Speech recognition grammars

Abstract: Grammar development for speech applications should not occur in isolation
               from the overall context of use defined by the application code and the end
               user. Since the grammar crucially defines the search space that the recognition
               engine will use, as well as the space of utterances that constrain the user, poor
               grammar design will lead to dissatisfied users and failed systems.   The
               successful grammar developer will be skilled not only in the development
               tools that are available, but also the principles of human-computer interaction,
               linguistic theory, paradigms of computational linguistics, and software
               development.

1.   INTRODUCTION

Just as "No man is an island" in the words of poet John Donne, so too is
no grammar an isolated artifact. In this chapter I wish to provide practical
guidelines for the developer of a speech recognition grammar.   These
guidelines are based on my experiences gained in writing numerous speech
grammars in a production environment at JustTalk, Inc, not a research
environment. What I mean by a grammar is, more precisely, *a set of
context-free phrase structure rules*, as are formally defined in both
linguistics and computer science [1-3]. In contrast, I do not address the
development of statistical-based grammar models as used in some speech
systems [4].

The process of developing a grammar for a speech application involves
far more than learning the syntax required by the interface to the recognition
engine and then stringing together a list of commands as if they constituted a

voice counterpart to a graphical user interface (GUI) drop-down menu. No user will accept a speech interface that implements the voice user interface (VUI) counterpart of a drop-down if there are more than a few choices. Imagine what you would do if you heard a speech interface that said, "Please speak your selection from the following list: Dasher, Dancer, Prancer, Vixen, Comet, Cupid, Donder, Blitzen, Rudolph." If you did not already have those names memorized then you would likely get both frustrated and impatient, and you would certainly become impatient if the list contained several dozen items.

Before writing a single grammar rule, the developer must consider the broad context within which that grammar will be used. That context includes the characteristics of the target user, the application code that will interact with the grammar, the system prompts that precede and follow user utterances, as well as the structure of the VUI itself.

In addition to these contextual matters, linguistic notions such as complexity, lexical and syntactic ambiguity, pragmatics and general principles of discourse also affect the grammar. It helps for the grammar developer to be familiar with linguistic issues such as Gricean maxims, conversational implicature, presuppositions and other concepts in semantics and pragmatics [5, 6] .

Theory impacts practice. Or at least it should.

The grammar defines the search space that the recognizer will employ to determine what the user said. How you design and develop that grammar will play a major role in the user experience and be critical in determining whether your system is successful or not. If you ignore the development guidelines below, you run the risk of wrecking what may otherwise be a nice speech grammar.

2. LIMITATIONS OF SPEECH GRAMMARS

In the field of speech recognition, the term 'natural language' apparently means whatever a company's marketing director wants it to mean. However, in every other field the term 'natural language' has a well-defined meaning. Whether it is Linguistics, Computer Science or Philosophy, the term 'natural language' simply denotes a naturally-occurring human language such as English, Russian or Navajo. It is this latter, technical sense that I will use when I write 'natural language'. Examples of languages that are not natural languages would be Esperanto and Java. These are generally referred to as artificial languages. And while it is tempting to describe VoiceXML as an unnatural language, I will resist that urge.

No speech application uses a complete grammar of a natural language such as English. Rather, every speech recognition application necessarily implements a subset of a natural language grammar, and any linguist would regard these grammars as miniscule – even trivial. The grammars are deliberately made as small as reasonably possible in order to maximize recognition accuracy. For example, if *only* a telephone number is expected in a user's utterance, there is generally no need for the grammar to recognize anything else with the exception of "universal" commands such as "help". To add additional utterances would be to increase the search space and allow the greater possibility of misrecognitions.

The application grammars are typically "chunked" by function, and swapped in and out by the application code as necessary in order to keep their size small, which also has the positive effect of reducing system latency for the user.

The basic goal of the grammar developer is to match the grammar as closely as possible to the utterances of the user at a particular point in the application flow, as shown in Figure 1:

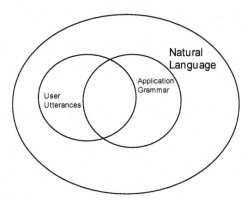

Figure 1. Linguistic Relationships in Speech Applications

Of course, the goal is to have the intersection of "User Utterances" and "Application Grammar" be equivalent to the union of those two sets, although in practice this is virtually impossible, in part because users both can and will say almost anything.

Assuming that we have determined the most common utterance types to build into a grammar for a state of the application, we still have a big problem in how to represent those items in a grammar that is both functional from the user's perspective and feasible from the developer's. This problem is significant because for any utterance *type* there is virtually an unbounded number of ways to say it syntactically. Take the example of "Prepare for the budget review with my team". Consider some of the alternative ways of saying the same thing:

– I have to prepare for the budget review with my team.
– Get ready for the budget review with my team.
– Budget review with team.
– Team budget review.
– Contact team members for budget review preparation.
– Call budget review with sales team.
– Group review of budget.

If we tried to capture all of these alternative utterances for every semantically important type, we would essentially return to the need for a complete syntactic grammar of the English language, which again is not possible.

3.   WHO IS THE USER?

Before any grammar development, before any design, before anything else is begun you must ask yourself who the expected user is. Just as you must know your audience before preparing a public speech, you must know your user before you can anticipate how they may speak. Some relevant questions to ask include the following:

Will users be trained or untrained? A voice portal with a toll-free phone number may be used by anyone, and the developer who assumes that users will have a mental map of their system is likely to end up with unhappy users. It is tempting to say that grammars for untrained portal users will be simpler than those for more sophisticated applications with paying customers who will undergo extensive training, but this is not necessarily the case.

Depending upon the sophistication of the underlying application, the portal grammar may in fact be more complicated. This could be the case, for example, if the grammar writer needs to accommodate a wide variety of optional utterances or syntactic variations for the less sophisticated user. It is again tempting to say that portal applications should employ directed dialog interfaces, but the untrained, occasional user may be more inclined to expect a mixed initiative dialog model since they will not likely know the limitations imposed upon them by the system.

How often will users be on the system? The daily user requires different support than the monthly user who is more likely to forget what the allowable utterances are.

How tolerant is the user expected to be? Users may be more tolerant with an application that provides a high degree of value than one with a lower value-added. This does not mean, of course, that the developer of the high-value application should be less attentive to user needs than for a low-value application. But it may mean that the high-value application can push the limits of usability in order to gain more functionality – hence value – than in a less valuable application.

All these questions and more will impact not only the grammar developer, but also the application code developer. Nothing can be done well until you understand the characteristics of your user, and this leads us to our first guideline for the grammar developer.

Guideline 1: Know your user.

Grammars are Situated in a Human-Computer Dialog System

Once you have an understanding of your user, you are ready to design the system VUI. When I refer to VUI design, I refer to what is often called the dialog design for every state of the application. The structure of the dialog flow between human and computer has a major impact on both the form and content of the grammars. Therefore, grammar design should follow VUI design.

I do not have the space to fully discuss VUI design, which itself is a book-length topic, so I will simply point out those aspects of VUI design that directly impact grammar design. Broadly speaking, the VUI can either follow a directed dialog philosophy or one that allows the user a less-constrained, semantically richer dialog, which may or may not be classified as mixed initiative.

By a directed dialog I mean one where the system is almost always in control, prompting the user for atomic utterances with limited semantic content, and moving to the next state to repeat the process. User utterances may or may not be confirmed. A partial example will illustrate the directed dialog approach.

System: This is the Acne Flight Reservation System. Please tell me your desired departure date.
User: (speaking on February 10, 2002): April first.
System: Do you wish to fly on April first, 2002? Please say either "Yes" or "No".
User: Yes.
System: Tell me the city and state for your departure.
User: Las Vegas, Nevada.
System: Did you say Las Vegas, Nevada? Please say either "Yes" or "No".
User: Yes.
System: Please tell me the city and state for your arrival.

User: Hoboken, New Jersey.
System: Why would you want to leave Las Vegas for Hoboken, New
             Jersey?

Figure 2. Dialog Fragment to Illustrate Directed Dialog

The directed dialog (with or without the sarcasm) may be a desirable
VUI paradigm for occasional users who will receive no prior training and
will not remember from one interaction to the next just what to say or how to
use the system. As suggested in *Figure 2*, the grammars in a directed dialog
system will normally be small with little complexity. Directed dialog is the
speech counterpart to a touch-tone interface. It accomplishes the task, but is
tedium incarnate.

A more natural VUI design might be possible for frequent users who also
may receive some training prior to first use. Given this type of user,
utterances that are semantically richer are possible, as long as the user knows
that they must still speak within the syntactic confines of the grammar. An
illustration appears in *Figure 3*.

System: This is the Acme Flight Reservation System. When would
             you like to travel?
User   (speaking on February 10, 2002): I'd like to travel on April
             first.
System: I will book you a flight for April first, 2002. Please tell me
             your departure and arrival cities.
User: Las Vegas to Hoboken.
System: Approximately what time would you like to leave Las Vegas,
             Nevada for Hoboken, New Jersey?

Figure 3. Non-Directed Dialog Fragment to Illustrate Semantically Rich Utterances

You can see that the grammars will need to be far more complex for the
semantically rich VUI than for the directed dialog VUI. For example, the
grammar for the second user utterance would likely allow for a great variety
of utterances, a small number of which are schematically shown in *Figure 4*.

from <departure city> to <arrival city>
<departure city> and <arrival city>
<departure city> to <arrival city>
departing from <departure city> and arriving in <arrival city>
<departure city> <departure state> to <arrival city> <arrival state>
from <departure city> <departure state> to <arrival city> <arrival state>
from <departure city> <departure state> to <arrival city>
to <arrival city> from <departure city>

arriving in <arrival city> from <departure city>

landing in <arrival city> <arrival state> from <departure city> <departure state>

etc.

Figure 4. Departure and Arrival Utterances

A hybrid between directed dialog and semantically rich systems is also possible. In the hybrid system, users may provide complex, semantically rich utterances, but they may also provide single, atomic utterances. In the latter case, the system prompts them for the missing information, as shown in *Figure 5*.

System: This is the Flex Flight Reservation System. When would you like to travel?

User (speaking on February 10, 2002): in April.

System: What day of April 2002 will you be traveling?

User: The first day.

System: I will book you a flight for April first, 2002. Please tell me your departure and arrival cities.

User: Vegas.

System: Departing from Las Vegas, Nevada and traveling to which destination?

User: Hoboken, Jersey.

System: Good choice.

Figure 5. Hybrid VUI

In the hybrid system, the more sophisticated user may have an experience much like the one in *Figure 3*. But for the novice user who only supplies the more limited types of utterances that are typical of directed dialogs, the system seamlessly falls into a directed dialog mode, prompting the user for each additional information element needed to complete the transaction.

Depending upon the expected users and other design considerations, a true mixed initiative VUI may be created whereby the users can wrest control from the system and direct the dialog according to their own needs. A mixed initiative system requires much sophistication on the part of the code developer as well as the grammar writer since far fewer constraints are placed upon the user. An example is shown in *Figure 6*. As all software developers are aware, users can and will do almost anything. In the context of a speech system, the type of dialog in this figure may not be common, but it may certainly occur.

System: This is the Intelligent Flight Reservation System.   When would you like to travel?
User: Somewhere around ten a.m.
System: What is the date of your trip at ten a.m.?
User: April first.
System: I will book you a flight for April first, 2002. Please tell me your departure and arrival cities.
User: I need to travel coach.
System: Please tell me your departure and arrival cities and I'll check for coach availability.
User: Las Vegas to Hoboken, and are there any discounts available?
System: Yes, there is one discounted seat available in coach class from Las Vegas, Nevada to Hoboken, New Jersey.

Figure 6. Mixed-Initiative VUI

You can see that the choices made in the VUI design will have a major impact on the types of utterances designed in to the grammars. This leads to our next guideline.

Guideline 2: Design the VUI before anything else.

However, even after VUI design the grammars can only be written in tandem with the system prompts to elicit an utterance from the user. The lexical choices and syntactic structures employed in the prompts are extremely significant and will influence the user's response, as much as the structure of questions in an opinion poll influence respondents' answers.

Prompt design is not easy, and even experts can design poor prompts. For example, the dialog fragment in *Figure 7* appears on the website of one of the major suppliers of speech recognition engines.

User: I want to speak to John.
System: We have two Johns at this office. Do you want John Smith or John Wesley Harding?

Figure 7. A Disjunctive Yes-No Prompt from a Speech Technology Supplier

The problem here is that the caller may barge in on this prompt after hearing the first name "John Smith" and say "Yes", which is an out-of-grammar utterance! Disjunctive choice prompts of the form "A or B" should never be expressed as a Yes-No question. This is not an isolated example. One recognized expert, who is frequently an invited speaker at speech conferences, has been noted to use a similar example of a disjunctive Yes-No prompt. He even commented during one talk that he had "cleverly designed the prompt to lead the user to say the correct thing."

Guideline 3: Design your prompts cleverly to lead the user to say the correct thing.

I recommend that immediately following the VUI design, the grammar developer create an initial design for all prompt-grammar pairs in the system, designing all help-error-timeout prompts as well (see below). Each entire grammar need not – and should not – be written at this time. A simple "stub" grammar of a small number of expected utterances will do.

Before these draft prompts and grammars are finished, the developer should determine if the prompt-grammar pairs are well matched, or if there are some unforeseen surprises such as in the disjunctive Yes-No dialog above. The simplest way to accomplish this is just to perform a "Wizard of Oz" [7] (WOZ) test whereby someone plays the part of the system and reads off the prompts, and another person plays the part of the user. The grammar designer should pick people not already familiar with the application, and should provide them with enough "training" so as to understand the basics of the application and their roles in the WOZ test, but should be careful not to coach the person playing the user or say anything to influence that person's unrehearsed responses to the system prompts. WOZ testing can catch many awkward or otherwise inappropriate prompts at little to no cost. The WOZ test should essentially traverse the whole VUI, not just the prompts and grammars, testing all proposed states. Such a test can often expose not only bad prompts and grammars, but also poorly designed VUI flow. Early detection of a poor design is far less costly than after the code has been developed, implemented and deployed to real users.

Guideline 4: Perform WOZ testing of your initial VUI, prompts, and grammars.

3.1 Application Code

The grammar interacts with the program code, and the two will constrain each other. Typically, the grammar returns a semantic interpretation of a user utterance, and that interpretation will be used by the application code to perform some action. Thus, the grammar's output is the code's input. However, the program structure may at times restrict the semantic return values. Software developers will typically write re-usable code objects. For example, they may write code objects to handle airline names and airline flight numbers, referencing a semantic structure that consists of a semantic feature-value pair such as, '(airline_name northwest)' and '(flight_number 1762)'. A typical prompt-utterance pair that results in the latter semantic structure might be: *System: What is your flight number? User: seventeen sixty-two.*

Now suppose that elsewhere in the VUI you have a prompt such as *System: Please say your airline and flight number,* expecting responses such as *User: Northwest flight 1762.* For this, you write a grammar that returns feature-value pairs that consist of airline and flight number, e.g. '(northwest 1762)'. However, your software developers may balk at this since they already have distinct code objects that handle airline names and airline flight numbers as cited above, and they want to reuse those code objects instead of writing a new one that combines the functionality. In this case, either the software developer or the grammar writer will have to accommodate the other.

Since the software is downstream from the grammar's semantic interpretations, the software developers are the *customers* of the grammar developer. I am of the opinion that customers are to be pleased, whether those customers are the external paying customers or the internal customers of data and information. Therefore, the grammar developer will save time, effort and grief by frequently communicating with the software development group, and taking the time to learn the architecture of their code.

Guideline 5: Know your developers and their code.

4.   GRAMMAR DESIGN

Earlier in Figure 1 I used a Venn diagram to illustrate how the utterances predicted by the grammar should ideally be coextensive with the set of actual user utterances. For anything other than a trivial grammar that can provide an exhaustive listing of these utterances, the grammar developer will need to make decisions about how to structure the space of utterances with subgrammars, i.e. sets of context-free production rules that comprise a hierarchy.

If the developer is trained with a linguistics background, then it is tempting to use syntactic based rules with non-terminal symbols (subgrammar names) like 'NounPhrase' or 'PrepositionalPhrase'. If the user is expected to give an imperative sentence as a command to the system, then such a rule hierarchy may look something like *Figure 8.* This notation is the standard one used in linguistics whereby optional constituents are indicated in parentheses and alternations are shown in curly brackets.

Imperative	→	TransitiveVerb (Pronoun) ObjectNounPhrase
TransitiveVerb	→	{say, tell}
Pronoun	→	me
ObjectNounPhrase	→	(PossessivePronoun) Noun
PossessivePronoun	→	my

Noun   → {airline, flight number}

Figure 8. Syntactic Grammar

There are difficulties with syntactic-based rule hierarchies in a speech grammar, besides the fact that the grammar in *Figure 8* over-generates (e.g. "Say me my airline"). Suppose that elsewhere you need a grammar that contains the transitive verbs "book" and "reserve". You now need to invent a rule with a different, albeit similar, name.

One alternative to this proliferation of syntax rules is to combine all of them into one common syntax rule, e.g. TransitiveVerb which contains all such verbs, and CommonNoun which contains all common nouns. But this is no answer because now your grammars will dramatically over-generate wherever they are referenced, allowing utterances like "Book my airline" where the user only wants to request a lookup.

This is more than a cosmetic problem of inelegance. There is a very real detrimental effect that will arise in having a purely syntactic-based rule system that over-generates for the context. For every such utterance that is in the set allowed by the grammar but not in the actual set of utterances likely to be said by real users, there is the possibility of that unlikely utterance being the matched utterance in a misrecognition. When the user says "Tell me my flight" there is a non-zero probability that the system will match and return the interpretation for "Book my flight". Such misinterpretations will lead to user confusion and the appearance of a system that violates the Gricean maxim of relevance.

This problem is inherent to any syntax-based grammar for large utterance search spaces. The solution lies in the use of grammars whose non-terminals represent semantic concepts, rather than syntactic constituents. A possible semantic grammar [8, 9] counterpart to *Figure 8* is shown in *Figure 9*.

LookupCommand   → Lookup (Pronoun) FlightInfoPhrase
Lookup   → {say, tell}
Pronoun   → me
FlightInfoPhrase → (PossessivePronoun) FlightInfo
PossessivePronoun → my
FlightInfo   → {airline, flight number}

Figure 9. Semantic Grammar

In effect, this solution is equivalent to using multiple versions of syntactic rules that are all named differently, according to their context of use. Using concept-based names for the rules is preferred over different versions of syntactic rule names because the semantics-based naming offers a self-documenting aspect that will greatly aid in grammar maintenance. This solution is not without its own set of problems, however. The primary difficulty is that a semantic grammar leads to a proliferation of rules that participate in similar syntactic relations. The developer trained in traditional linguistics will cringe at the thought of writing grammars that do not formally capture these generalizations. And for a very large application with very many such semantic grammars, maintainability will become increasingly difficult. Many verbs and many nouns may be duplicated across different rules.

However, the advantage of the semantic grammar is one of performance and usability which is of extreme importance to the customer, hence to the grammar developer at the speech software vendor which depends vitally upon end user satisfaction.

There is an opportunity here for vendors of grammar development tools to aid in the maintenance, as well as the creation of semantic grammars.

Guideline 6: Use semantic, not syntactic grammars.

5.   ERROR PROMPTS

I previously stated that all help prompts, error prompts, and timeout prompts should be developed soon after the initial VUI design. The error prompts are of particular relevance for grammar development. An error prompt is played if the system is unable to match the user's utterance. This may occur as a false negative; that is, the user has said something that is in-grammar, but the probabilistic nature of the engine resulted in failure to recognize that utterance. But it may also occur because the user really did say something that is out-of-grammar.

The default behavior for a recognition error condition in VoiceXML is to simply re-play the initial prompt. [3] However, it is more common for a system to play a context-dependent error prompt to the user, which can provide more information than the initial prompt. This error prompt can be followed by the original prompt or not, depending upon the VUI design.

In any case, there is an opportunity that should not be lost in the design of error prompts. Because common causes of recognition errors are out-of-grammar utterances, a good error prompt should provide information back to the user to help guide the user back in to the set of utterances defined by the grammar. Knowledge of the grammar is therefore crucial to the design of the error prompt, and it is the grammar developer who will likely design these error prompts.

As an example, consider a simple Yes/No grammar that expects the user to say either the single word "yes" or the single word "no". Likely out-of-grammar utterances resulting in error conditions would be various synonyms for these words such as *yeah, yup, absolutely* and *nope, not at all,* or even *huh-uh.* If the solicitation prompt were "Is this correct?" the user may even respond 'correct' or 'it sure is' as a synonym for 'yes'.

In the event of a non-recognition error, just replaying the solicitation prompt is likely to result in a repetition of the user's original out-of-grammar utterance. Thus, a good error prompt should guide the user as to what may have gone wrong. For example, one of the following error prompts may be more useful than the default solicitation prompt:

- Please say 'yes' or 'no'.
- Just say the single word 'yes', or the single word 'no'.
- I need you to say one of two words: 'yes' or 'no'.
- I can only understand the word 'yes' or the word 'no'.

Error prompts for more sophisticated grammars, as those shown in *Figure 8* or *Figure 9* for airline flight information, can be challenging. The prompt developer must balance informativeness of the prompt against the desire for prompt brevity. WOZ testing may be the best method to test and refine various prompts.

Guideline 7: Design error prompts to rein in out-of-grammar utterances.

6.   COMPLEXITY

Albert Einstein once said that "everything should be made a simple as possible, but not simpler." In general, this is good advice for the grammar writer, although it can be extremely difficult to practice. The grammar developer wages a constant war between expressiveness and simplicity. The more expressive a grammar is, the less simple. However, there are design decisions that can help mediate this war.

Some considerations that can help are rather subtle. I will mention one of them that involves the syntactic mood of the utterances defined by the grammar. *Whenever feasible, obtain user commands in the form of imperatives.* This constraint is followed in the JustTalk main menu, and elsewhere such as in the calendar and ToDo descriptions. One advantage with English imperatives is that the verbs are free of inflections. This reduces the search space for the recognizer, thereby reducing the potential for misrecognitions. An additional benefit is that it is relatively easy to *train* users to provide commands. This advantage cannot be understated. Reduction of the cognitive load upon the user is *extremely* important.

Another consideration that is rather obvious involves the use of directed dialog, which in general mitigates complexity. Of course, the tradeoff here is that the users may become frustrated if the VUI is too tedious. Again, there is a tradeoff between expressiveness and simplicity. Einstein understood this since he did caution people not to be too simple. Too much simplicity in a grammar results in a tedious VUI. One wants to achieve just enough simplicity to result in a productive user experience, while retaining enough complexity so as to give the illusion of free-form speech.

Guideline 8: Avoid complexity, but keep enough to amaze your users.

7.   AMBIGUITY

Most discussion I have seen in training materials and books on the topic of ambiguity in speech grammars focuses on utterances that have more than one parse path and which result in different semantic interpretations. For example, the Nuance documentation for grammar developers contains an example where the user utterance "Call John" can result in one interpretation of "Call John Smith" and another of "Call John Brown" because the grammar in the example has "John" as a synonym of both "John Smith" and "John Brown". Development tools exist to assist the grammar developer in locating such potential ambiguities.

These tools are well and good, and the usual care must be taken by the grammar developer to avoid such ambiguities. However, a far more insidious form of ambiguity can arise that directly relates to the fact that we are dealing with the spoken, rather than the written language. A commonly used example involves "how to recognize speech" vs. "how to wreck a nice beach." The ambiguity can only be evident when one says either phrase aloud, and then noticing how the other interpretation could arise. While this is the stereotypical example, the point drives home when you consider a real example from a real application.

At JustTalk, we developed a product known as *JustExpense* ™, which is an interface to an expense reporting system. When developing the prototype, our expense-entry grammar allowed users to say things like, "Set taxi to $20," In the grammar, the preposition 'to' was defined as an optional part of the utterance as was the word 'dollars'. Thus, one allowable utterance was "Set taxi to twenty." Notice that the juxtaposition of the preposition with the monetary amount creates an ambiguity in the *spoken* language that does not exist in the written language. This utterance could be (and sometimes was) interpreted by the recognition engine as "Set taxi two twenty" which then triggered a disambiguation sub-dialog to distinguish between "$2.20" and "$220", both of which were incorrect amounts with respect to the user's intent. The only possible recovery in those instances, was to complete the ill-advised disambiguation request, delete the incorrect entry, and retry. This could hardly be described as user-friendly.

Similarly, use of the optional preposition 'for' in another syntactic variant resulted in ambiguities with the number 'four', as in "Enter 20 for taxi." In this example, there was no disambiguation sub-dialog if a misrecognition occurred. The system simply entered the incorrect value $24 into the database. Since speech is probabilistic in nature, such misrecognitions could not be reliably duplicated and would have been a nightmare if this grammar had been put into production.

In an expense reporting application such misrecognition errors become critical. Hence for the production system, we changed the grammar syntax in order to avoid them. These kinds of ambiguities can be exceedingly difficult to detect because they only arise through the spoken language. The software tools to help identify ambiguities are of no assistance in detecting these kinds because they only arise through the *interaction* of the recognition engine with the grammar during a recognition event.

The inflectional poverty of English makes these kinds of spoken ambiguities fairly common, but they will be even more prevalent in languages like Chinese or Thai where inflectional morphology is non-existent and homophones even more numerous than in English.

This point is important for developers of systems that will be localized to other languages. Companies must be careful during such localization *not* to more-or-less translate grammars from source to target language. When the target language grammars are being developed, they must be created by persons who are trained in speech application development. If outsourced to a third-party localization vendor, disastrous results can be expected as the primary deliverable.

Another type of ambiguity to avoid is when the ambiguity exists in the language, but not in the application grammar. An example will clarify. One common grammatical ambiguity in natural language involves the concept of scope. For example, what is the scope of the adjective in the phrase "black Cadillac and Lincoln"? Does it mean ((black Cadillac) and Lincoln) or (black (Cadillac and Lincoln))? What is the scope of the negation in "no boys and girls"? What is the scope of the quantifier 'all' in "all dogs and cats"? Many such examples can be supplied.

The relevant point for speech recognition grammars is that if the developer's grammar only contains one of the interpretations, then chaos could result if the user has the other interpretation in mind when speaking. The system's behavior or response may not match the user's expectations. The ambiguity may not always be a problem, depending upon the application. For example, if the application is a speech-to-speech machine translation system, then scope ambiguity may carry directly across from the source language to the target language in exactly the same way that it does when humans are translating or interpreting. Even though "All dogs and cats" is ambiguous in English, it is equally ambiguous in German as "Alle Hunde und Kätze."

However, in most applications the developer needs to be extremely vigilant to be able to notice when the language is ambiguous but the application grammar is not. Again, there are no tools to help the developer here. Being a native speaker of the language does not suffice for linguistic competence when it comes to grammar development. It is only through relatively deep familiarity with natural language as is typically attained through a study of linguistics that the developer can avoid these traps, though extensive WOZ testing can sometimes help.

Guideline 9: Avoid ambiguity.

8.   MISCELLANEOUS

As a grammar developer, you will want to take full advantage of the tools available to you, including weights and probabilities [6]. After you have deployed your application and gathered usage statistics, this information can be used to determine how frequently certain paths in the grammar are followed according to user utterances.   You can improve system performance by converting this information to weights and probabilities which will favor more frequently-traversed paths. The result will be higher recognition accuracy, fewer misrecognitions, and more satisfied customers.

There are a variety of grammar development tools available from the speech recognition engine vendors, as well as third-party tools suppliers. If you will develop your system in VoiceXML, then there are two supported grammar syntaxes available to you. While the VoiceXML 2.0 specifications [10] state that all 2.0 systems must support the XML syntax for grammars, I would strongly recommend not attempting to write grammars in XML format. Use only the ABNF format, which the standard unfortunately only recommends, but does not require. *Table 3* will illustrate why you should only use the ABNF format. It shows two equivalent grammars that indicate the user may say one of three words, or may say other words stated in another grammar. Imagine trying to write any very large grammar using the chatty XML syntax, and I believe you will agree that the more compact ABNF syntax would be far easier to write and maintain.

Table 3. ABNF vs. XML Grammar Syntax

ABNF List of Alternatives	**foo | bar | baz |** **$anotherGrammar**

XML List of Alternatives	\<one-of>
	  \<item> foo \</item>
	  \<item> bar \</item>
	  \<item> baz \</item>
	  \<item>
	    \<ruleref
	      uri="# anotherGrammar"
	    /ruleref>
	  \</item>
	\</one-of>

Notation matters. If you need further convincing, then try to develop a large program in binary instead of a high-level language. Or try learning calculus directly from Newton without the benefit of Leibnitz' notation.

9. CONCLUSIONS

I hope to have convinced the reader that grammar development demands a high level of skill and attention to a wide variety of factors that impact both the form and the content of the grammar. These factors include grammar naming conventions, VUI design models, application software constraints, linguistic complexity and ambiguity, user characteristics, grammar tools and choice of syntax.

All of these factors and more will determine how closely your grammar matches user utterances. To the extent that the grammar correctly predicts these utterances, your recognition rates will go up, as will user satisfaction, adoption rates and ultimately your company's income.

REFERENCES

[1] A. Akmajian, R. Demers, A. Farmer, and R. Harnish, *Linguistics: an Introduction to Language and Communication*, 4th ed. Cambridge, MA: MIT Press, 1995.

[2] P. J. Denning, J. B. Dennis, and J. E. Qualitz, *Machines, Languages and Computation*: Prentice-Hall, 1978.

[3] A. Hunt and S. McGlashan, "W3C Speech Recognition Grammar Specification (SRGS)", W3C Proposed Recommendation, http://www.w3.org/TR/speech-grammar/, 2002.

[4] D. Jurafsky and J. Martin, *Speech and Language Processing: an Introduction to Natural Language Processing*: Prentice-Hall, 2000.

[5] P. Cole and J. Morgan, *Syntax and Semantics,* Academic Press, 1975.

[6] C.-K. Oh and D. A. Dinneen, *Syntax and Semantics,* New York: Academic Press, 1979.

[7] L. F. Baum, *The Wonderful Wizard of Oz*. Chicago, IL: George M. Hill Co., 1900.

[8] K. Godden, "Designing Large-Coverage Grammars for Speech Applications," presented at the Annual Meeting of the Applied Voice I/O Society (AVIOS), San Jose, CA.

[9] T. Winograd, *Understanding Natural Language*: Academic Press, 1972.

[10]   S. McGlashan, D. C. Burnett, J. Carter, P. Danielsen, J. Ferrans, A. Hunt, B. Lucas, B. Porter, K. Rehor, and S. Tryphonas, "Voice Extensible Markup Language (VoiceXML 2.0)", W3C Proposed Recommendation, http://www.w3.org/TR/voicexml20/, 2002.

Chapter 7

Designing for Speaker Authentication

Judith A. Markowitz
J. Markowitz, Consultants

Key words: speaker authentication, speaker verification, speaker recognition, biometrics,
              voice-based biometrics

Abstract: Since September 11, 2001 there has been a sharp increase in the use of
              biometric-based security, including speaker authentication. Some of the
              guidelines for developing usable speaker authentication dialogs correspond to
              basic principles that apply to the design of good speech recognition
              interactions. Developing effective speaker authentication dialogs for security
              also demands attention to considerations that are distinct from – and
              sometimes contrary to – those used for speech recognition.

1. INTRODUCTION

The terrorist attacks perpetrated against the United States on September 11, 2001 spawned a sharp increase in interest in and use of biometric-based security. Among the technologies of special interest to government and private industry is speaker authentication: technology that uses features of a person's voice to verify that that person is, indeed, who she or he claims to be.

The aim of this paper is to provide a solid foundation for building effective speaker authentication dialogs. Guidelines for constructing usable speaker authentication dialogs include many of the basic principles that govern creation of good speech recognition interactions, but the two are not identical. Speaker authentication dialogs that provide effective security demand attention to considerations that are distinct from – and sometimes contrary to – those used for speech recognition.

1.1   The Speaker Authentication Family

Speaker authentication is a biometric-based security process. It belongs in a category called *speaker recognition* or *voice-based biometrics*. Voice-based biometrics are the most diversified and complex of biometrics. As *Figure 1* indicates, one reason for this is that speaker recognition is part of two larger families: speech processing and biometrics.

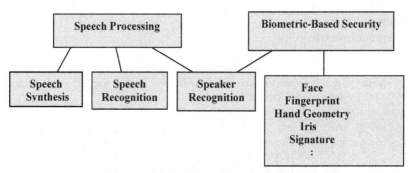

Figure 1. Speaker Recognition Family Tree

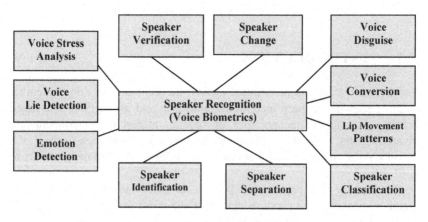

Figure 2. Speaker Recognition Techniques

A closer look at the speaker-recognition category (*Figure 2*) reveals that it includes a large number of technologies.

The two most highly commercialized speaker-recognition technologies are *speaker verification* and *speaker identification*. Speaker verification uses voice samples to determine whether a person is who she or he claims to be. It always involves a one-to-one match between a voice sample taken from the claimant and a voice sample that is known to be from the person whose identity is being claimed. In contrast, the object of speaker identification is to assign an identity to the voice of an unknown speaker. To accomplish that, speaker identification compares a voice sample taken from the unknown person with samples from two or more known individuals.

Speaker authentication does not appear in *Figure 2* because it is not a separate technology within this grouping. It is usually synonymous with speaker verification, but also includes one-to-many comparisons (speaker identification). Incorporating both approaches allows an organization to maintain consistency in its authentication procedures despite varying conditions. For example, a bank that uses the account number as the password for telephone banking or other services can extend that format to joint accounts.

1.2 Biometric-Based Security

Figure 1, above, revealed that one of the families to which speaker authentication belongs is biometric-based security. Biometric-based security includes a broad spectrum of traits that can be used to identify individuals. Law enforcement has a long tradition of using bite patterns, footprints, tattoos, and scars to help identify criminals. Recently, a masked bank robber in Australia was identified by his distinctively knobby knees.

Unlike knobby knees, some biometric characteristics are generic attributes that can be used across populations of individuals. The most well known are fingerprints and DNA. This paper is only concerned with fully- or semi-automated authentication tools, many of which are used for security or monitoring.[1]

Biometric-based security fits into a larger schema of approaches to authentication for security. The standard categorization is shown in *Table 4.*

---

[1] The term *biometrics* has an entirely different meaning in medicine where the definition refers to the process of measuring physiological features. Consequently, reference to a fingerprint or voice as a biometric has no meaning but a measurement of a voice parameter would.

Table 4. Type of authentication for security

Method	Examples
What you have	Authenticates something you possess (card, key, badge)
What you know	Authenticates personal/secret information (PIN, ID, password, mother's maiden name)
Where you are	Authenticates your location (home-incarceration bracelet, GPS system)
Who you are	Authenticates a personal attribute - biometrics (voice, face, iris, fingerprint)

As *Table 4* indicates, biometric-based authentication is the only form of authentication that is direct. All other approaches authenticate through indirect means (e.g., through possession of a card, or knowledge of a password).

1.3   Speech Processing

The closest relative to speaker authentication in the speech-processing family is speech recognition. Speech recognition is a class of non-biometric technologies that identify the words and phrases in an utterance. It cannot identify or verify speakers and is basically uninterested in speaker attributes – except as a way of improving its ability to recognize what is being said. In fact, most speech recognition systems work hard to eliminate speaker-linked information. Consequently, the use of speech recognition – by itself – for security is equivalent to manual input of passwords (what you know authentication) and lacks the power of biometric security. At the same time, knowledge about what a person is saying can enhance the performance of speaker authentication and shorten authentication interactions.

2.   SPEAKER AUTHENTICATION DIALOGS

2.1   Basics

There are two steps in biometric authentication: *enrollmen* and *authentication*. The purpose of enrollment is to obtain one or more biometric samples that can be tagged with the identity of the enrolling individual. Features needed to differentiate one person from another are extracted from the samples and stored as that person's *reference model* (also called *reference voiceprint* and *speaker model*).

The authentication process begins with an *identity claim*. Traditionally, identity claims consist of presenting the system with a card, token, password, or PIN but a growing number of systems are using automated methods, such as the ANI of the caller's telephone, for the identity claim. Others may use a passive biometric, such as face recognition, to provide an initial identifier. Once the claim has been made, the authentication system retrieves the reference model for that identity and obtains a spoken sample from the claimant. That sample is compared with the reference model and generates a *matching score*. Generally, if the score is better than a pre-defined *threshold* the identity claim is accepted. Otherwise, the person is identified as an *impostor*. One of the emerging dialog issues in speaker authentication deployments is the variability that can be applied to the identity claim and the final acceptance or rejection of the claimant.

Speaker authentication supports several basic kinds of interaction: *text dependent, text prompted*, and *text independent*. One of the first decisions a developer must make is which of these dialogs will be used (or will be the primary dialog). Considerations include the time required to complete enrollment and authentication, the obtrusiveness of the process, incorporation of additional security, the use of speech recognition, and the likelihood that criminals will attack the system using recordings.

2.2 Text-Dependent Dialogs

Text-dependent systems base their analyses on models of the speaker saying a pre-determined password or ID, such as an employee ID, an account number, or even their own names.

Figure 3 and *Figure 4* display two variants of typical text-dependent dialogs.

Figure 3 obtains an identity claim that is input manually using the touchtone keypad of the caller's telephone. Then it requests the caller's password. *Figure 4* shows the same dialog with speech recognition

> **System:** *Using the touchtone keypad, please enter your*
>
> *employee ID number*
>
> **User:**   Enters *321455*
>
> **System:** Retrieves reference model for 321455
>
> **System:** *Please say your password*
>
> **User:**   *Open sesame*

Figure 3. Text-dependent dialog – manual identity claim

> **System:** *Please say your employee ID number*
>
> **User:**   *321455*
>
> **System:** Uses speech recognition to identify the digits
>
> Retrieves reference model for 321455
>
> Compares the utterance with the reference model for 321455

Figure 4. Text-dependent dialog — spoken identity claim

2.2.1 Strengths

Traditional text-dependent authentication parallels familiar password procedures and is, therefore, easy for users to understand. It is often multi-factor authentication because it combines a biometric (the voice) with knowledge (the password) and/or something you know/have (the identity claim).

Enrollment and authentication are generally short which is often desirable for commercial authentication. Most systems need only three or four repetitions of a two-second password to enroll a new speaker. Enrollment can be done unobtrusively if speech recognition is used and the password is something the individual expects to say, such as their name, ID, or an account number. Unobtrusive enrollment may easily extend over multiple calls. The advantage of multi-call enrollment procedures is that it allows the system to get more caller and telephone-channel information.

Authentication usually requires one utterance of the password. The use of spoken input reduces the traditional two-step (ID claim + authentication) process to one step. Even though the procedures are short, usability and user acceptance are enhanced by enrollment and authentication dialogs that specify the approximate number of utterances that the user should expect to supply.

2.2.2 Weaknesses

Today, many people are becoming overloaded with passwords and PINs, some of which are bizarre alphanumeric and symbol patterns that change on a regular basis. Lost, stolen, and forgotten passwords are commonplace. Any password – even familiar phrases – can be forgotten. Consequently, depending upon the nature of the authentication phrase, text-dependent systems may need password-reset procedures.[2]

If spoken input is obscured by noise or if there are other quality problems, an enrollee may be asked to supply more than three or four samples and a claimant may need to provide more than one utterance for authentication. Dialogs are needed to request additional utterances and to transfer to a backup strategy when samples continue to fail quality checks. Repeated requests for more samples can annoy or anger users consequently there should be a limit to the number of such requests. As with any biometric, there are individuals who, for some reason, cannot be enrolled or consistently authenticated. Consequently, dialogs need to be careful to avoid blaming the user for any difficulties.

Unobtrusive authentication is desirable from a usability perspective but it raises the issue of privacy. In all instances where this approach is used it should be done with the caller's full knowledge and approval. Dialog design for these systems needs to include a short statement about the existence of the biometric system, a method for obtaining initial approval, and additional help regarding the privacy protections involved. The legal department of an organization may need to be involved.

In theory, text-dependent authentication is vulnerable to recordings. In practice, the vulnerability of these systems to tape-recorded attacks depends largely upon whether the tool includes *liveness testing* and *anti-spoofing* technology for detecting the acoustic signatures, distortions, and other features associated with recordings. This reporter from the *Boston Globe* did his best to defeat a text-dependent system with anti-spoofing.

I had a couple of people call the system and try to use my pass phrase one male, one female. Neither could get in.

Then, I tape recorded myself saying my pass phrase as I gained access to the system. I could gain access while I was doing the recording but when

---

[2]   Ironically, password reset, itself has become an automated process that often employs speaker authentication.

I played it back to the system, no dice. Its polite-but-firm response: "Hmm, that didn't sound like you."[3]

2.2.3 Password Selection

The first decision to make regarding passwords is whether to allow users to select personal passwords (*user-defined*), assign passwords, or to employ the same password for everyone (*global* or *universal password*). User-defined are less likely than assigned passwords to be forgotten but they may not supply the acoustic information needed to perform accurate authentication. Consequently, systems with user-defined passwords should have functions for evaluating the acoustic properties of a proposed password and dialogs for describing good passwords.

Assigned passwords are certain to have the necessary acoustic properties for good authentication but they are more likely to be forgotten than user-defined passwords unless they are items that the caller expects to say, such as their name or account number. Global passwords are rarely used. When they are they are less likely to be forgotten, but often bring with them greater dependence on the identity claim. Global passwords are most useful when the password is the name of the organizations (e.g., *Verification by Chemical Bank*). Metro One, a supplier of directory assistance and specialized call-processing services, uses *Infone*, the name of the service, as its global password and based the identity claim on the ANI of the caller's telephone. When the ANI does not match an Infone subscriber a Metro One operator will ascertain the identity claim and then transfer the caller to the Infone system for speaker authentication.

Some systems employ multiple passwords. The additional passwords serve as backup when the matching score obtained during authentication is too close to the threshold level. Multiple passwords are also useful when there are varying levels of security. A user may be asked to supply two or more passwords for a moderate- or high-security task. Other approaches, sometimes called *knowledge verification*, may be implemented. Those are discussed in the section on Advanced Techniques, below.

2.3   Text-Prompted Dialogs

Text-prompted (also called *challenge-response*) systems enroll multiple items. During authentication, the system randomly selects from among the enrolled items (or generates new items from them) and asks the user to repeat them. *Figure 5* displays a basic text-prompted dialog.

---

[3]   Kirsner, Scott *Boston Globe* April 7, 2003. p. C15

System: *Please enter your employee ID number*
User: Manually enters *321455*
System: Retrieves reference model for 321455
System: *Say forty-two fifty-nine*
User: *forty-two fifty-nine*
System: Compares the utterance with the reference model for 321455

Figure 5. Typical text-prompted dialog

Text-prompted technology is often used with offenders in community-release programs, such as home incarceration. Those systems often call the offender so that an identity claim is implicit. When an offender calls one of these systems it obtains and examines the ANI of the telephone to ensure that the caller is where she/he is supposed to be.

2.3.1 Strengths

Text-prompting is highly resistant to tape-recorded attacks because impostors cannot know which items will be requested. This establishes a level of variability that renders use of tape recorded material extremely difficult. Furthermore, some systems that enroll digit strings (e.g., 14325) further enhance resistance to recordings by recombining the enrolled digits into strings that were not in the enrollment sequences. One commercial product uses its acoustic models for speech recognition and internal dictionary to support the generation of unenrolled phrases. It might, for example, enroll a number of city-state pairs, such as *Chicago, Illinois*, and use the acoustic data from those items to prompt for *Washington, DC*.

There is no password-reset problem in a text-prompted system because the system instructs the person to say specific items. The PIN or other ID, if used, may still be forgotten.

As *Figure 5* indicates, other than the text-prompted items the language in the dialog can be extremely simple. The items themselves are generally not complex but some users need even greater simplicity. DUI offenders are a good example. Because they tend to be non-violent, they may be placed in home-incarceration programs. If they are in advanced stages of alcoholism they may not be able to respond to digit strings or other types of standard input and it may be necessary to adapt the vocabulary to very familiar words, such as family names.

2.3.2 Weaknesses

Most users are annoyed by the long enrollment and authentication procedures required for text-prompting. As a result, text prompted is not well-suited to customer applications, unless the customers understand and welcome the enhanced security provided by these systems. Criminal offenders in community-release programs may not be bothered by the length of the interactions. One reason is that a speaker authentication program is preferable to being incarcerated and may afford them greater personal movement than an ankle bracelet. They may not, however, feel that way when the system calls them at 3 a.m. asking for authentication.

Since being placed in a speaker authentication program is often a privilege that can be revoked, some offenders feel extra pressure to succeed. This can produces stressed speech patterns for authentication that are not present during enrollment – even when the offender is enrolled on his/her home telephone. In such cases, the dialog can do little to alleviate the problem, but enrollment procedures can be modified to capture stressed speech patterns by adapting the enrollment process so that the offender does not know when enrollment ends and authentication begins.

2.4   Text-Independent Dialogs

Text-independent systems ask or expect a person to talk so that what the person says is different every time. Most existing deployments of text-independent technology listen in the background to a conversation between a call-center agent and a caller. *Figure 6* displays an example of such a background system.

Caller:	*I want to transfer $1million to my offshore account*
Agent:	Turns on speaker authentication *What is your account number?*
Caller:	*3214557789*
Agent:	*Mr. Jim Jones?*
Caller:	*Yes*
Agent:	*I will need to verify some information. Please tell me your social security number.*
Caller:	*111-22-3333*
Agent:	*What is the other name on this account?*
Caller:	*My wife, Jenny Jones.*
System:	to agent *Caller identity verified*

Figure 6. Text-independent authentication in the background

2.4.1 Strengths

Text-independent speaker authentication is the only approach that can be done entirely unobtrusively. Both enrollment and authentication can be performed in the background while the person is engaged in another activity, such as speaking with a call-center agent. If the acoustic data are gathered while the person is engaged in another activity no formal automated are needed to elicit spoken materials for authentication. If the process is used with the person's active participation, a dialog may be created to gather additional pieces of information that may assist an agent or a speech recognition system. Some systems have dialogs that ask users to repeat an utterance that is rich in acoustic content. Those dialogs are not as meaningful to users and are less desirable.

2.4.2 Weaknesses

It is more difficult to accurately compare utterances that are totally different from each other. This problem can be reduced by gathering more acoustic data. Consequently, text-independent enrollment and authentication are longer than for text-dependent technology. Most commercial systems require a minimum of 30 seconds of speech[4] or do the enrollment unobtrusively during multiple calls.

Unobtrusive use of text-independent authentication raises the privacy spectre. The relationship between privacy and technology is highly emotional and characterized by conflicting agendas (some of which are hidden or partially hidden) and contradictions. Privacy has already been broached as a concern tied to the very use of biometrics and in response to proposals for creating a centralized biometrics database for government use. In addition, there is no reason to assume that regulations restricting the recording of someone's communications do not apply to recordings of people interacting with text-independent technology (or speech recognition systems for that matter) — even though the recording is not used for any purpose other than authentication.

When faced with a need to record communications, other industries, such as call-centers in financial-services institutions and help desks, have established a policy of informing customers their calls may be recorded or monitored. Some institutions allow callers to request their calls not be recorded. Privacy issues can be lessened by storing only digitized, processed models rather than the original analog recordings and by obscuring the link between a model and other information about the speaker. If such privacy-enhancements are implemented it may be useful to provide a monologue describing them.

---

[4] Thirty seconds is much longer than it seems. For example, the first half of Abraham Lincoln's *Gettysburg Address*, shown below, or the first eleven lines of Hamlet's famous "To be or not to be" soliloquy, spoken at a natural, unhurried pace is approximately thirty-seconds long.

> Fourscore and seven years ago our fathers brought forth on this continent a new nation, conceived in liberty, and dedicated to the proposition that all men are created equal. Now we are engaged in a great civil war, testing whether that nation, or any nation so conceived and so dedicated, can long endure. We are met on a great battlefield of that war. We have come to dedicate a portion of that field, as a final resting place for those who here gave their lives that that nation might live.

3. ADVANCED TECHNIQUES

The combination of speech recognition and speaker authentication has already been presented as a way to shorten text-dependent interactions. The amalgamation of the two technologies also offers a number of additional benefits that can be employed to enhance authentication performance and flexibility.

3.1 Utterance verification

Speech recognition may be used to verify internally that an individual has said what the system expects them to say. *Figure 7* provides a simple example.

System:	*Say your account number*
User:	*1234 Billy! You leave your sister alone!*
System:	Uses speech recognition to identify the digits
System:	*I'm sorry. I didn't hear that. Please say your account number*
User:	*1234774*
System:	Uses speech recognition to identify the digits
	Compares the utterance with the reference model

Figure 7. Speech recognition for internal verification

In this example, speech recognition enabled the system to determine that the user did not say a valid account number and re-prompted the caller for the number. By itself, text-dependent speaker authentication would not have been able to distinguish between invalid input and an impostor and could have produced an erroneous authentication rejection (called *false non-match* or *false rejection*). Internal verification is also useful when the person makes an error. It would, for example, alert a text-prompted system if a person responded with *12347* when prompted for *12447*.

3.2 Multiple thresholds

A threshold represents a minimum level of correspondence between a reference model and a new voice sample that is required in order for a claim of identity to be accepted. Normally, biometric systems use one threshold.

Sometimes more than one threshold is needed – especially for systems that expect input from a spectrum of telephone handsets and channels. An upper threshold can be set at a level which reflects a high-degree of confidence that the caller is who he/she claims to be. A lower threshold can be set to reflect a high degree of confidence that the caller is an impostor (possibly after the content of the utterance has been verified). Matching scores falling in the area between the two thresholds can generate re-prompts in text-dependent and text-prompted systems, use of other authentication, transfer to a human, or another solution.

Products are beginning to utilize multiple thresholds to support *variable length authentication*. These systems continue to request additional information/input until a specified overall confidence level (for rejection or acceptance) is achieved. The associated re-prompting dialog should be short and the number of requests needs to be constrained before some action is taken (e.g., transfer to a human).

3.3 Knowledge and Intelligence

Some systems ask callers to supply answers to specific questions as part of enrollment or as the entire enrollment procedure. For example, a text-dependent system may pose questions like *What is your favourite color?* and *Where were you born?* during enrolled to use as backup when the matching score is inconclusive. For example, an extended authentication of this sort procedure might be invoked when an authentication score judged to be too close to the threshold, to support higher levels of security, or as strong authentication (knowledge factor) in noisy conditions.

A text-prompted system may be configured to engage in a Question-and-Answer dialog for enrollment and authentication. During authentication, the system might elicit answers to one or more randomly-selected enrolled questions.

Speech recognition could be used to analyze the content of the input for either approach. Speaker authentication might also be called upon to provide additional voice authentication analyses.

Higher-level knowledge is starting to appear in advanced systems for human-human and automated interactions. These systems supplement text-dependent or text-independent biometric verification with questions whose answers are derived from account and database information. These answers are interpreted using speech recognition and may include dynamic/changeable information, such as telephone numbers. The final determination is based on the combined results of model matching and knowledge. These dialogs are longer but can be structured to access information that the caller deems a natural and expected part of the interaction.

4. HANDLING ERRORS AND PROBLEMS

No biometric technology of any type is 100 percent accurate. Like all biometrics, speaker authentication systems make *false rejection* and *false acceptance* errors. An important factor in error generation is the placement of the threshold that is used to determine whether an identity claim will be accepted or rejected. The threshold determines how close the match between the reference model and the new input must be for a claim of identity to be accepted. That is, it determines how sensitive the authentication decision is to variability. All biometrics must handle variability[5]. For speaker authentication variability includes channel and background noise, use of different telephones for enrollment and authentication, and hoarseness.

4.1 Rejection

When the matching score is below the threshold level the system rejects the person as an impostor. If the threshold is set so that it limits the amount of variability that is allowed, slight variations between samples from the same person may generate scores that fall below the threshold. When this occurs, the system has generated a false rejection error (also called a *false non-match* or a *Type I* error). False rejection errors are often easy to detect because rejected users generally complain.

Some false rejection errors can be eliminated through the use of noise cancellation, channel noise detection, speech recognition to verify that the person said the proper words/phrases, model adaptation, or other technologies that operate in the background.

Such tools can reduce the number of false rejections but are unlikely to eliminate them entirely. There may be instances when the system determines

---

[5] Each kind of biometric has its own kinds of "noise" and variability. Fingerprint systems, for example, can be affected by dirt, dryness, differences in the positioning of the finger. Iris scan and face recognition systems are affected by glare and different orientations of the head. Like speaker recognition, the performance of face recognition systems is affected when different cameras are used for enrollment and identification. Most other biometrics use proprietary sensors so variation in the input device is not a factor at this time.

the quality of the input is not good enough to process[6] or the *anti-spoofing* function detects a recording.

Whether the user is transferred to a human, the authentication process is lengthened, (e.g., a different type of speaker authentication is used, knowledge verification is invoked), or another type of security is applied, the system needs to alert the caller to a change in the usual authentication procedure. Usability and customer satisfaction research has found that users respond best to short rejection-statements that place no blame on them.

4.2   Acceptance

When the score is above the threshold the person's identity claim is accepted. A speaker authentication system commits a false acceptance error (also called a *false match* or a *Type II* error) when it accepts the model of an impostor as valid. Positioning the threshold to handle greater variability between models of the same person makes the system less likely to generate false-rejection errors but renders it more vulnerable to accepting clams made by good impostors[7]. Unfortunately, successful impostors are unlikely to announce their achievements, but it is possible to utilize backup or transfer procedures when the score is close to the threshold, too good[8], or otherwise suspicious. Dialogs for those situations can be identical to those used for authentication rejection.

4.3   People Who Cannot Use Speaker Authentication

For every biometric there is a segment of the potential user population that cannot use it. The most obvious group of non-users for speaker authentication is people who cannot speak. The population extends to individuals whose voices are extremely hoarse, speakers whose models are too variable to create consistent models, and people who speak very softly. Such individuals are usually identified at the time of enrollment.

Handling non-users entails design of enrollment and authentication procedures that do not iterate ad infinitum in a futile attempt to get sufficient data to create a model. Enrollment and authentication can be structured to

---

[6] This is called *failure to acquire*. When failure to acquire occurs during enrollment, it is called *failure to enroll*. Failure to acquire and failure to enroll are problems experienced by all biometric tools.

[7] It is possible to position the threshold so that it generates an *equal error rate*. That is, the same percentage of false rejection errors as false acceptance errors.

[8] Some systems check to see whether the new input resembles the reference model or a recent authentication model too closely. If this is the case, a very high quality recording may be suspected.

detect problems quickly and to transfer the individual to a help desk or system administrator who can determine the probable cause of the problem. As with rejection communications, a statement associated with the transfer should not blame the user for the interruption of the process.

5. FINAL WORDS

Speaker authentication dialogs adhere to many of the basic usability principles that govern dialogs for speech recognition. Those principles include clarity, brevity, and the ability to quickly detect and resolve problems.

At the same time it should not be forgotten that speaker authentication is security: a line of defense against attacks. The authentication procedures need to reflect the security requirements associated with the systems and functions that the speaker authentication is protecting (e.g., accessing bank account information, performing a transaction, getting into a secure area of a facility, monitoring a home-incarcerated felon).

The opposing pulls between customer service and security will influence the type of speaker authentication that is selected, threshold setting, and the dialogs that are developed for those systems.

PART 3

DEPLOYMENT

Chapter 8

Using VoiceXML 2.0 in the VxOne Unified Messaging Application

Robert Keiller
VoxSurf

Key words: VoiceXML 2.0, Unified Messaging,   UI configurability, template-based page
              generation, model-view-controller

Abstract: This article describes VoxSurf's experiences using VoiceXML 2.0 to build
            and deploy the VxOne Unified Messaging application. Several of the issues
            encountered in developing this application are discussed including the
            generation of dynamic pages, with particular reference to customer
            configuration of the UI, speed and latency of the application and prompt
            generation.

            On the basis of our experience we conclude that VoiceXML 2.0 is set to
            become the standard platform for delivering voice applications and legacy
            IVR replacements. However, to be an effective development language for
            applications that need to support high degrees of configuration and re-use,
            developers will additionally need to engineer:

            • separation of UI and data

            • abstraction of the UI for flexible configuration

            • developer tools to manage the abstracted resources and simplify
              application development

1.   INTRODUCTION

1.1   General

This article describes VoxSurf's experiences using VoiceXML 2.0 to build and deploy the VxOne Unified Messaging (UM) application. This is a fully featured voicemail and email solution available via voice, HTML and WAP with the voice persona written using VoiceXML 2.0 [1].

1.2   Contents

An overview of VxOne is given in Section 2. Subsequent sections describe some of the lessons learnt from the application and suggestions for the use of VoiceXML. The areas covered are:
Section 3: the generation of dynamic VoiceXML pages;
Section 4: speed and latency issues;
Section 5: prompt generation;
From our experience we conclude in Section 6 that VoiceXML 2.0 is set to become the standard platform for developing voice applications and legacy IVR replacements.

1.3   VoiceXML 2.0

This article assumes some familiarity with the VoiceXML 2.0 specification (see http://www.w3.org/TR/voicexml20/).

2.   OVERVIEW OF VXONE

2.1   Summary of features

The VxOne IP based Unified Messaging application allows common messaging services such as voicemail and email to be brought together into a single place and accessible from one telephone call or web session. Access can be through whatever device is the most convenient, so that users can use an ordinary telephone, a WAP or i-mode enabled mobile phone or a standard HTML browser to access their messages. This is made possible by a model-view-controller architecture in which different access modes operate on a common data model that integrates with the mail store via the IMAP and POP protocols.

VxOne is provided as a Java servlet application to landline and mobile phone operators to run on any VoiceXML 2.0 compliant voice browser. Operators can completely change the look and feel of the user interface for their requirements, e.g. to replicate a legacy voicemail platform or to provide a fully featured voice activated unified messaging solution.

Key features of VxOne are:

- **Connection to multiple email account(s):** Users are not restricted to email accounts provided with the service but can register multiple legacy email accounts provided they support the POP3 or IMAP interfaces.
- **Fully integrated with** HTML **and WML email clients:** In particular voicemails can be retrieved via the HTML client or downloaded direct into third party email clients such as MS Outlook.
- **VoiceXML 2.0** compliant: The voice persona of the application is fully VoiceXML 2.0 compliant and has been tested against several browsers including Motorola, VoiceGenie, PipeBeach, VeraScape and Nuance voice browsers.
- **Personal address book for** sending **messages:** In the voice application new messages can be sent to any contact in the address book. Contacts can be uploaded from MS Outlook using the vCard protocol. LDAP can also be used to upload contacts from enterprise subscriber databases.
- **Full read/reply/forward/delete and new message ability from any device:** In the case of messages sent via voice, a recorded message is sent as a wav file attachment to the email.
- **HTML based account maintenance:** In addition to the full email reading capability, the HTML pages provide account maintenance including:
    adding new email accounts;
    adding contacts to the address book;
    registering telephone numbers that can be used to access the application without needing to enter the account ID;
    setting advanced user preferences (see Section 5).
- **Fax forwarding via WAP, PC, or Voice:** Emails, including their attachments, can be forwarded to any fax machine.
- **Notifications via SMS of newly** arrived **voicemail and email:** Users can be notified via SMS of all new voicemails and all new emails matching user defined filtering rules.
- **IMAP filtering:** Users can specify message filters to apply to IMAP accounts in order to speed up access to certain messages. This is particularly useful in voice where browsing through junk emails can be time consuming.
- **Calendar and tasks support:** Users can review their personal calendar and task lists on Exchange 2000 servers.

- **Configurable UIs:** Prompts and grammars are configurable separately from the abstract call flow and can be redefined by customers. VxOne can be deployed as a voice-only solution, as a DTMF only solution or as a mixed mode solution.
- **Multiple deployment options:** The application can be configured for the following deployments:
email only (for email reader services);
voicemail only (for legacy voicemail replacement);
UM (email and voicemail);
UM linked to a voice portal.
- **N-tier support:** VxOne has full n-tier support for multiple domains. Within each domain the application can be configured differently so that subscribers can have different look-and-feels for the HTML pages or hear different sets of recorded prompts in the voice application. In particular this provides for multiple branding of the application in an ASP environment and support for differentiating between classes of service.

2.2 Overview of voice dialogs

A simplified overview of the voice application dialog flow is given in *Figure 1*.

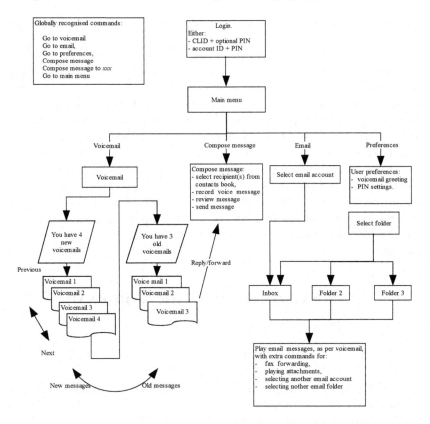

Figure 1. Overview of default dialog flow

2.2.1 Default UI

VxOne is provided with a default UI based on VoxSurf's own testing experience but can be reconfigured according to customer's requirements (see Section 3).

Style

The default VxOne UI is aimed at frequent users who want to access information quickly. Such users soon become familiar with barge-in and the main commands to operate the application. The dialog therefore consists of a straightforward menu-based, system directed dialog supplemented with a small number of global commands (e.g. "go to email", "go to voicemail", "compose a message to John Doe"). The grammars used are small, generally accepting just the command words with possibly one or two alternatives but no attempt is made to understand free, natural speech as users are expected to become familiar with the application's commands. Help prompts always list the main options and are also played if there are repeated noinput or nomatch events.

Barge-in

Barge-in is always provided, except on a small number of feedback prompts (e.g. "going to email") which play while the next page is being fetched. To improve usability in noisy environments hotword bargein is used throughout. This reduces the frequency of interruption by background noise which testers have found to be frustrating and sometimes confusing.

DTMF

DTMF input is always accepted as an alternative to speech but the DTMF options are kept out of the main voice prompts. To hear the DTMF options users can press *0, and a reference to this is always added at the end of the voice help prompts. Keeping the DTMF help prompts separate in this way enables the normal voice prompts to be kept relatively short and concise.

3. GENERATION OF DYNAMIC VOICEXML PAGES

3.1 MVC architecture

The VxOne architecture is based on the MVC architecture and implemented using Java servlets:
1. The **model** consists of Java classes representing the user's profile and
  – application sessions for email, voicemail and, where deployed,
  – application sessions for calendar and tasks.

These classes are not voice specific and are re-used by HTML and WML access channels.
2. The **controllers** implement the call flow on a coarse-grained level, e.g. ,
  – the links between major components:
  – links between top-level components;
  – fetching next/previous email message;
  – sending a composed message and returning to previous dialog.

Finer grained implementation of the call flow is performed by the VoiceXML pages themselves. When a URL request is received from the voice browser, the controllers handle the request and select an appropriate view to be returned.
3. The **views** consist of VoiceXML pages constructed by the controllers in response to requests from the VoiceXML browser.

There is no absolutely clear-cut distinction between which parts of the call flow are implemented by the controllers and which by the VoiceXML pages. A balance is made between:

using small pages with almost all the call flow implemented on the server and requiring many page fetches which can be inefficient due to the extra network traffic and the overheads of client-server communication;

using large pages with few page fetches which can be inefficient due to the need for the VoiceXML browser to parse unnecessary VoiceXML.

Where possible VoiceXML pages in VxOne perform a distinct dialog unit, such as the playback of an email or voicemail message, or the composition of a new outgoing message. Larger dialog units which contain optional or repeated components may be broken down into multiple pages with the use of VoiceXML subdialogs.

This article is primarily concerned with the generation of VoiceXML views.

3.2   Views

Each VoiceXML page is itself comprised of three distinct parts that form a microcosm of the MVC model:

abstract call flow – fine grained control of the call flow (e.g., the order in which collection of one or more data entries is made, such as the recipients of a message, the recorded message itself and any delivery options; the logical handling of user input via <filled> and <block> elements where this is not handled by the controllers);

presentation skin – the UI that is applied to the call flow (e.g., how the content of a message is presented; the prompts played in an input field; the prompts played for noinput and help behaviour);

application data – data obtained from the main model that is to be presented to the user (e.g., a message being reviewed including subject, recipients, received date, message content).

The processes involved in the generation of VoiceXML pages by VxOne are shown in *Figure 2*.

3.2.1 Call flow development

The abstract call flow is encapsulated in a VoiceXML template. This template is created during application development using VoiceXML with the following VoxSurf modifications:

Output prompts (i.e. those giving the user information such as the contents of an email or voicemail message) are specified as abstract prompts by

writing an <audio> element with a vxsaudiokey attribute that is resolved
to a concrete prompt when the presentation skin is applied.

Likewise <grammar> elements have a vxsgrammarkey attribute.

All fields have vxsclass and vxsid attributes, and normally no <prompt>,
<help>, <noinput> or <nomatch> event handlers are specified at this
stage.

An ID attribute is supported on <var>, <assign>, <script>, <audio>,
<script>, <grammar>, <submit> and <subdialog> elements.

These modifications to VoiceXML are used by the application server at
run time to add the presentation skin and user data to the pages before
rendering the pages to the voice browser. NB all VoxSurf-specific features
are removed from the pages before sending to the voice browser.

Once created, the templates are compiled into java classes implementing
the W3C DOM interface using Lutris Enhydra XMLC. This allows powerful
programmatic manipulation of the XML Document Object. In addition
XMLC compilation also creates direct accessor methods for all elements
with an attribute of type ID.

Most configuration of the UI can be made via configuration of the
presentation skin (see Section 3.2.2), but more extensive modifications of
the UI that require call flow changes can be made by changing and
recompiling the templates. Alternative, customer modified templates are
supported via a Java factory pattern.

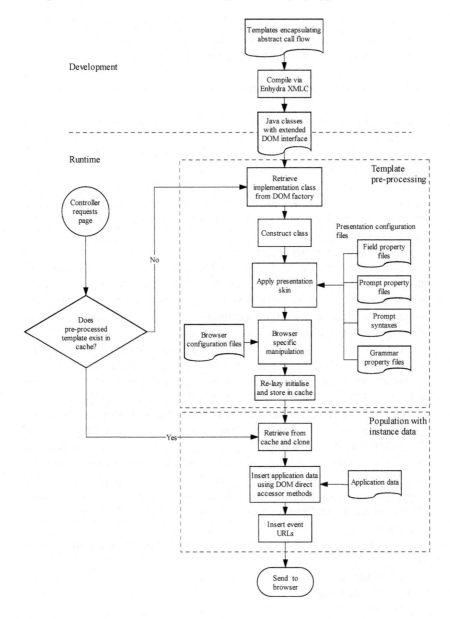

Figure 2. Generation of dynamic VoiceXML pages at run-time

The generation of a VoiceXML page from the templates at run-time is a two stage process:

template pre-processing, during which the presentation skin is applied and
   any required browser specific modifications are made;
population of the page with instance data each time the page is required.

3.2.2 Template pre-processing

The pre-processing of the template performs two functions:
1. application of the presentation skin;
2. performing generic browser specific manipulations that adapt the pages
    to the voice browser.

These processes are performed by the application server only once for
each template, the first time the page is required by any user. Because these
processes are applied only once, relatively expensive DOM processing
techniques can be used at this stage.

Application of the presentation skin

An essential feature of VxOne is the ability to apply different user
interfaces on top of a common call flow. This gives telco operators the
ability to take the off-the-shelf VxOne UI and customise it for different
languages, to replicate a legacy voicemail UI or to fit in with the UI style of
other components within a voice portal.

VoiceXML does not itself provide good mechanisms for supporting
multiple user interfaces. Maintaining separate VoiceXML templates for each
UI would entail major problems with maintenance and upgrade paths and
provide no re-use of VoiceXML between different user interfaces.

Therefore we have defined our own mechanisms for separating the UI
from the abstract call flow. It allows us to maintain a single set of
VoiceXML templates configured into a specific UI by flat configuration
files. These configuration files are easier for customers to edit and maintain
than VoiceXML templates. They also support hierarchical definition of
properties such that property definitions can be inherited from platform
default definitions and can be over-ridden only as required on a property by
property basis.

The presentation skin is defined by a set of presentation configuration
files:
field configuration files;
prompt definition files;
prompt syntax files;
grammar files.

Field configuration

The field configuration files define:
−   The number and style of prompts required for each field (e.g., the prompt
    counts − whether tapered prompting is required and if so, how many

levels – and whether separate prompts are required for DTMF and voice input modes);
- The handling of noinput, nomatch and help events (e.g., the prompts to be played, the event counters and the error behaviour on repeated noinput or nomatch);
- VoiceXML properties to be applied to the field (e.g., prompt timeout, interdigittimeout, termchar, etc);
- Extra links to be added to the field (e.g. go to main menu, transfer to operator).

The field properties can be defined either on a per field basis or application wide based on the vxsclass attribute of the field. Application wide definition of properties allows for rapid and consistent modification of the style of the user interface. The vxsclass attribute takes one of three values:
- menu: for menu-style fields (e.g. "please select from ...");
- data: for fields taking data entries (e.g. PIN, account and telephone number fields);
- boolean: for fields expecting a yes/no response.

Prompt definition

The prompt definition files map abstract prompts with vxsaudiokey attributes to concrete implementations of the prompt. These attributes can either be mapped to a single audio file or to a prompt syntax.

Prompt syntax

The prompt syntax files define a sequence of prompts that should be played out in place of an abstract prompt. Syntaxes may include VoiceXML <if>, <elseif> and <else> elements to select the prompt based on VoiceXML variables. Prompt syntaxes are expanded into the templates in place of the abstract prompts. Where syntaxes that include <if>, <elseif> and <else> logic are expanded into field context rather than executable context, expr attributes are used on <audio> elements to contain the necessary ECMAScript tests, e.g.:

```
<if cond="test">
    <audio src="audio.wav">
</if>
```

would be expanded as:

```
<audio expr="test ? 'audio.wav' : undefined">
```

This is effective but cumbersome and inefficient. Nested <if>s must be flattened to a sequence of <audio> elements each of which repeats the same set of ECMAScript tests.

Grammar

The grammar property files map vxsgrammarkey attributes to actual implementations of the grammar. Implementations for voice grammars differ depending on how many variants of the command are supported; implementations of DTMF grammars differ on the basis of the mappings between DTMF keys and actions. Where DTMF grammars are supplied there is an option in the field properties to generate automatically concatenated prompts such that the DTMF prompts always match the key mapping of the grammar (e.g. the mapping between actions and key presses in the prompt "to listen to your voicemails press 1, to change your user settings press 2" would be updated automatically if the grammar is changed).

Presentation skins applied via the presentation configuration files can be radically different. We have for example applied the following skins to the same set of templates:

1. The default UI;
2. A presentation skin for a voice-activated UM deployment that supports:
- Two input modes: voice + DTMF and DTMF only;
- Separate prompts for the input modes, with two sets of prompts defined for voice input and a single set of prompts defined for DTMF;
- DTMF prompts concatenated at run-time from the key mappings in the DTMF grammar;
- A multi-lingual DTMF-only presentation skin for replication of a legacy voicemail system with a single set of prompts used in each field.

Browser specific manipulation

Browser specific manipulation of the VoiceXML pages handles both non-compliances with the VoiceXML 2.0 specification (these are now rare in the browsers supported by VxOne) and non-standard extensions to the specification. Non-standard extensions are used particularly for audio control (pause, rewind, fast forward). These extensions are added to the templates and need to be removed for the voice browsers for which they do not apply.

Re-lazy initialisation

XMLC uses a process of lazy initialisation to speed up conversion from the java class to the text sent to the browser. This lazy initialisation stores the original text corresponding to the elements of the document so that when the document is converted to text all unchanged elements can be retrieved directly and the DOM tree only needs to be traversed for those elements that have changed. For large documents where only a few elements are changed, the use of lazy initialisation can speed up the conversion to text by a factor of 10 or more.

Unfortunately the initial preparation of the page changes almost the entire document, so the advantage of lazy initialisation is lost. Therefore we have modified the XMLC package to re-lazy initialise the document after the initial preparation of the page is completed. After re-lazy initialisation, the prepared pages are stored in a cache. When a particular instance of a page is required, it is retrieved from the cache and cloned. The clone is populated with instance data and returned to the voice browser. When the view is written out the DOM tree only needs to be traversed for those elements that have changed in the population with instance data.

3.2.3 Population with instance data

Each time a page is served, instance data is added to pages using direct accessor methods created by XMLC for elements with an attribute of type ID. For example, to set the messageNumber variable to 1 in a VoiceXML page, an attribute of type ID would be added as follows:

```
<var name="messageNumber" ID="MessageNumberID"/>
```

Then the server side manipulation of the DOM object representing the page would be:

```
dom.getElementMessageNumberID.setAttribute("expr", 1);
```

The use of direct accessor methods greatly speeds up the generation of VoiceXML pages because the need for DOM traversal is removed.

Direct accessor methods are also used to rewrite servlet URLs in <script>, <grammar>, <audio>, <submit> and <subdialog> elements so that the servlet can identify and process dynamic requests for these resources.

3.3   Discussion

3.3.1 Configurability and reuse through abstraction

For VxOne a single code base must be able to accommodate different configurations of user interface, call flow and application logic. Configuration of server-side Java code to support call flow and application logic configuration can be accommodated with standard OO abstraction techniques such as Factory/Strategy patterns. Java also provides mechanisms for reuse of code through standard inheritance and composition. However, the presentation language of VoiceXML does not provide equivalent mechanisms for abstraction.

The separation of the presentation skin from the abstract call flow logic provides a highly configurable architecture with which the same underlying core VxOne application can be configured to meet widely differing deployment requirements. Importantly much of the configuration can be performed by telco operators themselves.

The further separation of data from the VoiceXML pages allows for highly efficient generation of the VoiceXML pages.

3.3.2 Abstraction leads to increased complexity

The template based approach to developing VoiceXML is highly flexible and provides developers with the full expressibility of VoiceXML. Compared to VoiceXML tools-based approaches it also allows quicker development of work arounds to browser issues and makes it easier to make use of browser specific extensions. However, the resultant architecture is highly fragmented with the following interdependent components being brought together at runtime:

- VoiceXML templates
- Grammars
- Prompt syntaxes
- Java servlets receiving URL requests and inserting instance data into VoiceXML pages.

These components are not only used by developers but also by customers to configure their deployments. This means that configuration changes must be done safely and any errors must be detectable by the customer's own testing, not just by factory testing of the application.

3.3.3 Development and configuration tools

Whilst VoiceXML is a good target language for delivering highly portable voice applications, it is less good as a robust source language as there is very little, if any, checking of the data passed around within pages (VoiceXML has some very weak constraints requiring the use of <var> to declare variables). The most common problems are:

- ECMAScript expressions used within pages which refer to non-existent variables.
- Data inserted into <script>s by the application server which do not match variables expected by the template and/or prompt syntaxes.
- Unexpected slot names and/or values returned from grammars to VoiceXML pages and onwards to the application server.

These can lead either to VoiceXML error.semantic errors or to application side exceptions which are only discovered at run-time. Testing all branches of the call flow to find such errors is a very laborious process. In our deployments to date, much of the time spent in debugging configurations of the application has been to fix problems of this kind.

We are currently in the process of developing tools to assist robust configuration of the application. Currently these tools support:

- Verifying the existence of all external resources (audio files and grammars)
- Automatic conversion of grammar files between different grammar specifications.

To these we plan to add tools that will statically verify all ECMAScript references within our pages. To aid this process additional markup will be required to defined data interfaces between components. These tools will greatly accelerate product development via the template based approach by providing the equivalent of compile time variable checking in a VoiceXML page.

4.   SPEED AND LATENCY

Many of the responses from initial user testing of VxOne concerned the speed of the application. Delays in accessing data that are acceptable in an HTML application were deemed unacceptable for telephone based applications.

The time taken to access information is determined by two factors:
1. the dialog required to reach the data;
2. the delays in generating VoiceXML pages.

Both of these factors were examined closely to improve the speed of the application.

There may also be delays caused by the client side parsing of VoiceXML pages. These may eventually be reduced by using static VoiceXML pages with parsed DOMs cached on the voice browser.

4.1   Dialog

A number of small improvements were made to the dialog flow to reduce delays in accessing the application including:

Changing the log-in process: Users can now be identified by their calling number if they call from a pre-registered phone. Optionally they can then also bypass the need to enter a PIN. Since mobile phones are more personal than land-line phones, some users may choose not to use a PIN when calling from a mobile but will wish to enter a PIN when calling from a land-line phone.

Moving key information up to the main menu: Generally the most important piece of information that users want to know when they enter the application is the number of new voicemails and emails. This information was moved up, to come before the main menu prompt so users can get this information without having to select voicemail or email. (NB the number of emails is only given for the user's "primary account" which is held on a local mailstore because there can be substantial delays in accessing remote mail stores.)

Allowing configurability of the starting point: Some users want to use the application primarily for voicemail and want to enter voicemail immediately on log-in. Others want to use the application mostly for retrieving email and wish to go straight to email, possibly to a selected email account on log-in. User configurability of the application is therefore provided so that users can select where they wish to start.

Allowing configurability of email and voicemail headers: Originally the application always played the message number, the sender where available, and the received date of messages before the message content. Some users found this information helpful, others found it delayed the application too much. Therefore user options have been added to allow users to select which headers they wish to hear.

Re-recording and trimming of prompts: Some small speed improvements were made by re-recording some of the key voice prompts in a faster tempo and aggressively trimming silence from the start and end of the prompts. Also where prompts were concatenated to insert a variable number, e.g. "You have" + "2" + "new emails", whole prompts were recorded for numbers up to 10, so that concatenation/splicing delays were removed.

4.2   Delays in VoiceXML page generation

The dynamic page generation mechanism described in Section 3 reduces the time taken to construct a VoiceXML page from application data to a few milliseconds. Far more significant therefore is the time taken to determine the application data for a page. In VxOne the major delay in determining the application data for a page is retrieving email content from a mail server. Because users can register any legacy email account, the retrieval of email content can require contacting an arbitrary email server anywhere on the internet. This can result in significant delays which are beyond the control of the application.

To mitigate the effects of these delays VxOne preloads emails wherever possible. Thus, for example, while the browser is playing the first email in an account, the server will be retrieving the second email.

On occasions even preloading emails cannot prevent significant delays. If similar delays were to occur on an HTML browser, the user would eventually abandon the request and browse another page instead. In VoiceXML 2.0 there is no way (other than hanging up) for a user to stop a page request that is in progress. To avoid this situation VxOne always generates a "polling response" if a page request is not completed within 5 seconds. This "polling response" plays an explanatory message e.g., "Please wait while I download the email message". During this prompt the user can say "stop" to cancel the current request. If the user says nothing a new request is sent to the server to retrieve the originally requested page. Again if there is a further five second delay another polling page will be sent, this time with a shorter message "please continue to wait or say 'stop'". This continues until either the user chooses to stop the current request or the requested page is sent to the browser.

4.3   Static VoiceXML pages

The separation of instance data from VoiceXML pages can be taken to its logical conclusion by making the VoiceXML pages fully static and using the application server to deliver only the data to populate the pages.

Using VoiceXML 2.0 this is theoretically achievable using <script> or <subdialog> elements to retrieve data. Subdialogs will be required to fetch data where the fetch requires parameterising with client side data, since <script> does not support expr or namelist attributes whereas <subdialog> does.

In practice there may be problems with cookie support for dynamic grammar fetches (since URL rewriting is not possible with static VoiceXML pages, cookie support is required to associate all resource requests with user sessions) and the VoiceXML 2.0 specification is unclear as to whether ECMAScript objects may be returned from subdialogs.

With the current draft proposals for VoiceXML 2.1 [2], these problems can be avoided as both <script> and <grammar> will support expr attributes. Additionally there is a <data> element that may be used instead of <script> to retrieve data in an XML document.

If data is separated from VoiceXML pages in this way, significant performance gains on the client side become possible if voice browsers maintain an internal cache of parsed VoiceXML pages. When a new page is required, rather than loading the page from the web server and parsing it, a freshness check is all that is required before reusing an already loaded and parsed page.

5.   PROMPT GENERATION

An area in which the VoiceXML 2.0 specification has proved somewhat awkward in developing VxOne is the controls for browser side generation, selection and control of prompts, in particular:

- absence of for loops to iterate over an array of data items;
- absence of audio control to pause, fast forward or rewind the prompt queue;
- absence of if-elseif-else logic for field prompts.

5.1   Iteration over arrays of data items

This problem arises where the application needs to play back an array of items in a prompt, e.g. the recipients list of a message, and where the dimension of the array is not known when the VoiceXML document is produced. Using VoiceXML 2.0 a loop can be constructed to playback such a list using a self-clearing block, e.g.:

```
<var name="i" expr="0"/>
<block cond="i !=document.someArray.length">
    <prompt><value expr="document.someArray[i++]"/></prompt>
</block>
```

This will usually work, though on occasion it may fall foul of a browser's loop detection algorithms.

In the VoiceXML 2.1 specification a new <foreach> element is proposed which should fully address this situation.

5.2   Audio control

Many voicemail applications provide the ability to pause, fast forward and rewind a voicemail message. VoiceXML 2.0 provides no facilities to do this and it is necessary to use platform specific extensions, where available, to provide this.

The VoiceXML 2.1 draft specification provides audio control via the <mark> element and the markname and marktime properties of the application.lastresult$ object. This can be used to provide audio control if the application server applies offsets to audio files retrieved via URL requests to which the marktime attribute is added as a URL parameter.

However, this approach becomes very cumbersome where multiple audio files are queued together (e.g. audio files to play the date and time at which the message was received, the sender of the message and the message content itself). It also provides no audio control for TTS prompts.

5.3   if-elseif-else logic in field prompts

It is frequently desirable to playback only the list of currently active options in a menu. For example, in voicemail applications the option to call back the sender of a message may be presented only if the sender left a call back number. In more complex cases where several options may be inactive at one time it soon becomes desirable to use if-elseif-else markup to define prompts.

However, the <if>, <elseif> and <else> elements are only permitted in executable context, not as the children of field prompts. If prompts are moved into executable context, then prompt counter semantics are no longer supported. The only alternatives are:

– Apply the prompt selection logic server side;
– Make extensive and inefficient use of the cond attribute on <prompt> and the expr attribute on <audio> (see Section 3.2.3).

Applying prompt selection logic on the server side is inconsistent with the use of prompt syntaxes to configure prompts and also with VxOne's long term aim of moving to static cacheable VoiceXML pages. Therefore VxOne uses the second approach although this is not entirely satisfactory on account of the inefficient VoiceXML code that is generated.

6.   CONCLUSIONS

6.1   A powerful language for delivery of telephone applications

VoiceXML provides the most flexible technology available today for the delivery of voice applications over the telephone. In particular VoiceXML offers the following potential benefits to application service providers and developers:

– a powerful language for writing complex voice applications;
– a choice of platform vendors and platform independent applications, so that operators are not tied to a single platform;
– a re-usable skill set for developers, taking advantage of existing web development skills;
– freedom for developers from the need to control telephony, ASR and resources.

Current VoiceXML browsers go a long way towards delivering these business benefits to telcos.

Particularly significant for portability has been the development of the VoiceXML 2.0 specification. VxOne is written in VoiceXML 2.0 and is portable across several VoiceXML 2.0 browsers. The draft VoiceXML 2.1 specification will improve VoiceXML further in a few selected areas including fetching scripts and grammars via dynamic URLs. These changes will allow the development of applications that reside in browser memory as parsed DOMs, potentially increasing application performance. VoiceXML 2.1 also addresses some problems with prompt generation by allowing iteration over arrays of prompts. However some problems remain with audio control and conditional prompting.

6.2 VoiceXML development is potentially error prone

As a development language, however, VoiceXML can prove tricky to work with. Part of the problem is that, for a presentation markup language, VoiceXML 2.0 is very complex. The specification contains a large number of elements but pages still tend contain a much larger number of tags than the equivalent HTML page.

Much of this complexity in VxOne is down to the need to keep applications responsive by reacting to user input within the page. This requirement also explains the highly scripted nature of VoiceXML where scripting and the data model are implemented as ECMAScript.

Unfortunately ensuring ECMAScript expressions are correct becomes time consuming as there is effectively no type checking. We hope that development tools will in future provide assistance to reduce time spent resolving ECMAScript errors.

6.3 VoiceXML does not provide sufficient abstraction of UI

VoiceXML provides some abstraction between call flow and UI by having audio prompts and grammars as separate resources. However this in itself is not a sufficient level of abstraction for a commercial application that requires extensive customer specific reconfiguration of the UI.

The VxOne architecture for generating VoiceXML pages clearly separates call flow logic, user interface and data. Of particular note is the separation of the user interface definition into a presentation skin which is configurable post-deployment by telco operators. This enables re-use of the core VxOne application in a wide variety of environments.

REFERENCES

[1] S. McGlashan, D. C. Burnett, J. Carter, P. Danielsen, J. Ferrans, A. Hunt, B. Lucas, B. Porter, K. Rehor, and S. Tryphonas, "Voice Extensible Markup Language (VoiceXML 2.0)", W3C Proposed Recommendation, http://www.w3.org/TR/voicexml20/, 2002.

[2] M. Oshry, P. Baggia, M. Bodell, D. Burke, D. C. Burnett, E. Candell, J. Ferrans, J. Haynie, H. Kilic, J. Kusnitz, S. McGlashan, R. Marchand, M. Migdol, B. Porter, K. Rehor, and L. Ricotti, "Voice Extensible Markup Language (VoiceXML) 2.1", http://www.w3.org/TR/2004/WD-voicexml21-20040323/, 2004.

PART 4

NEW IDEAS

Chapter 9

Building a Standards and Research Community with the Galaxy Communicator Software Infrastructure

Samuel Bayer
The Mitre Corporation

Key words: dialog, standards, software infrastructure

Abstract: The best and most robust software standards emerge from a community of
              developers working in both academic and industrial settings. This community
              does not arise automatically from large research programs, but must be
              carefully supported. In the context of the DARPA Communicator program, we
              show   how   the Galaxy Communicator Software Infrastructure (GCSI)
              fostered the development of such a community.

1.   INTRODUCTION[*]

With the advent of powerful, commercially available speech recognition engines, it's been possible over the last several years to begin to take seriously the idea of rich, mixed initiative spoken interaction with automated agents. It is well-known that such interactions require a range of capabilities: speech recognition and synthesis, parsing and generation, and dialog

[*] The author would like to acknowledge all the other members of the MITRE DARPA
Communicator team for their substantial contributions to the work described here. This
research was funded by DARPA ITO under Army Prime Contract Number DAAB07-01-
C-C201. In addition, the software described here would not have been possible without
the generous contributions of the MIT SLS Group (http://www.sls.lcs.mit.edu), which
provided its initial implementation, joined MITRE in releasing it and MITRE's extensions
under a liberal open source license, and continues to be actively involved in its design and
use.

processing (e.g., [1, 2]). As we've progressed in building such systems, we've grown to recognize some of the ways in which these systems can be modularized, and how these modules can be configured and connected to each other.

As the market for these dialog capabilities has grown, the community has begun to develop and propose standards for some of these components. The W3C Voice Browsers working group (W3CVB) [3] , for example, has been active in standards development for speech recognition and synthesis, parsing and interpretation, and dialog. At the same time, there are programs in the research community which are attempting to extend the scope of capabilities of dialog systems. One such program was the DARPA Communicator program [4]. DARPA Communicator focused on pushing the boundaries of capabilities in cooperative, mixed initiative dialogs between humans and computers, and as a result was focused on much longer-range issues than the W3CVB working group is. The ideas emerging from programs like Communicator are immature, and thus by definition not ready for standardization. However, in the ideal situation, these ideas ought to coalesce into agreed-upon conventions which can feed directly into standards activities.

In this chapter, we will describe the underpinnings of the DARPA Communicator program which facilitate such a process, as implemented and realized in the Galaxy Communicator Software Infrastructure (GCSI). In Section 2, we'll describe the general problem of establishing the sort of engineering community we need. In Section 3, we'll introduce the GCSI and briefly describe its strengths. In Section 4, we'll discuss in detail those aspects of the design of the GCSI which facilitate the development process we're looking for. In Section 5, we'll summarize some remaining implementational and logistical details concerning the usability of the GCSI. Finally, in Section 6, we'll expand on the relationship among the GCSI and GCSI-compliant systems, standards efforts like W3CVB, and commercialization.

2.   ENABLING AN ENGINEERING COMMUNITY

The Galaxy Communicator Software Infrastructure is a distributed, message-based, hub-and-spoke infrastructure for dialog system construction. As such, it is not unique; for example, the Open Agent Architecture [5], the TRIPS infrastructure [2], and the TRINDI toolkit [6] can be characterized in this way. As with those infrastructures, the GCSI has been used by a range of sites to field a number of successful prototype systems (see, for example, [7-11]). In this paper, we will assume that architectures of this sort, and the

GCSI in particular, have been amply demonstrated to enable the construction of flexible spoken dialog systems, and we will not discuss how to do that here.

Rather, this chapter is about what happens after that: how to move from the functionality provided by such infrastructures to a community of researchers, students and developers, and finally to an agreement on standards. In this chapter, we will suggest that the GCSI is extremely well-positioned to facilitate such a process.

2.1 A successful engineering community

The best and most robust software standards emerge from a community of researchers, students and developers who can converge on these standards over time, using functional and testable implementations. This community needs to exercise all the aspects of these emerging conventions; so if, for example, the target of standardization is speech recognition or speech synthesis, community members need to test the configuration of these components and their run-time control. It's probably essential that these components be used by community members besides those who built them, since in this way the community will be forced to test unanticipated uses of these components. Similarly, if these components have a base of overlapping consumers, there are opportunities for comparing different approaches to comparable problems and for "best practices" to emerge.

The health of such a community depends in large part on the diversity of its members. Experienced researchers and developers must participate, and not just as representatives of academic institutions and pure research labs; engineers and scientist from commercial companies will test the state of the art by integrating emerging ideas with current products, or by field-testing prototypes of entirely new systems. In addition, such a community needs to support the process of training and educating new researchers and developers, both in industry and academia. Ideally, then, such a community would be able to leverage its components and end-to-end implementations as educational tools *and environments.* In this situation, students and trainees can experiment in the sorts of environments they'll encounter after their training, and they can be exposed to as wide a range of environments and different approaches as possible.

2.2 The challenge of large research programs

However, a community such as this does not necessarily emerge spontaneously from a large research program. The demands of progress in research emphasize functionality and research results over code sharing, and favor large institutions which are capable of building end-to-end systems consisting of locally-developed components. In those situations where sites share code among themselves, there's no inherent pressure to solve the code-sharing problem in a general way. As a result, in most cases, the developers of these software components are the only users, and the components are neither tested by others nor compared to each other.

The standards process is not the only process which suffers in such a situation. Sites which don't have the resources to develop most of the components themselves are at a considerable disadvantage; although they may be qualified to make major contributions in a particular area, they are limited in how they can participate. And since the number of large sites with the resources to build end-to-end systems is small compared to the number of small sites which might be able to contribute, this situation potentially excludes the largest portion of the potential community.

Similarly, students in educational institutions are limited, by and large, to the dialog systems developed by their local groups. If they're lucky enough to have such systems, they're limited in the variety of techniques they're exposed to; if they're not lucky enough to have such systems, they go without. As a result, both the number and variety of educational programs is limited.

Finally, without the dissemination of these tools and environments, smaller commercial developers lose valuable access to emerging research ideas, and are excluded from participating in the development process. As a result, a valuable source of feedback to the research community is lost.

Our challenge, then, is to "lower the bar to entry" for these smaller research and engineering sites and educational institutions, in order to have the best chance of building the community we seek. This means getting as many people involved as possible, at the lowest possible cost. We want to do this in a way which imposes minimal limitations on the form of the emerging conventions, but also makes it as simple as possible to compare competing conventions and identify the most successful. The chosen strategy will have to provide enough sufficiently efficient functionality that working prototypes (and, ideally, even products) can be developed. Finally, this strategy will ideally be low-cost enough that large participants will adopt it as well.

2.3   A concrete example of the problem

In [12], we describe a demonstration we developed to help illustrate the capabilities of the DARPA Communicator program. In this demonstration, we exemplified the initial steps involved in constructing end-to-end connectivity for a dialog system:

1. achieving audio I/O connectivity (by echoing the user's audio input)
2. incorporating speech recognition and synthesis
3. incorporating language parsing and generation

In addition, we chose to incorporate multiple speech recognizers and synthesizers and switch between them at run-time. This demonstration is illustrated in *Figure 1*.

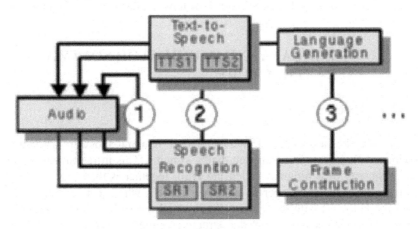

Figure 1. MITRE's Communicator demonstration

Assembling this demonstration presented the following problems, which are representative of the sorts of problems that a typical member of the community might face:

1. Only two of the components in the demonstration (the audio software and the language generator) are MITRE-made. The recognizers, synthesizers and parser are all produced by other sites. We were committed to modifying these components as little as possible, if at all.
2. The two speech recognizers produce different outputs. The output from recognizer #1 is lower case, and contains XML-like markup to indicate pauses and sentence delimiters; the output from recognizer #2 is in upper case, and contains no markup.
3. The two speech synthesizers interpret input strings differently. One doesn't know how to interpret XML, so it spells out any markup it finds, while another ignores it. One synthesizer treats capitalized words as acronyms and spells them out (e.g., "MITRE" is rendered as "M I T R E"), and one does not. As a result, the various recognizer-synthesizer pairs in path 2 in *Figure 1* will yield a range of behaviors, some of them undesirable.

4. The two synthesizers respond to and produce messages with differing names and structures; similarly for the two recognizers.

An infrastructure which makes it easy to navigate these incompatibilities at run-time is certainly one which will make it easier for a community to train students, share modules, construct end-to-end systems, and explore issues of "best practice" which lead to successful standards. In the remainder of this paper, we describe GCSI, and show how it addresses these issues.

3.   THE GALAXY COMMUNICATOR SOFTWARE INFRASTRUCTURE

3.1   Overview

The GCSI is a distributed, message-based, hub-and-spoke infrastructure optimized for constructing spoken dialog systems. This infrastructure, at its core, consists of a program called the **Hub**, together with a server library which allows the developer to construct servers which can communicate with the Hub and with each other. Servers and the Hub communicate with each other using named key-value structures called **frames**. These frames form the basis of all structured communication in the GCSI.

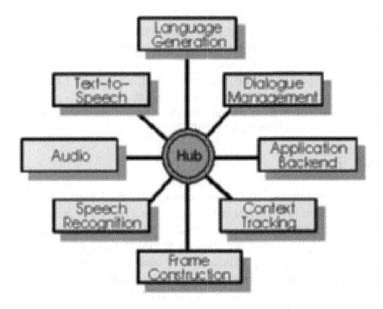

Figure 2. A sample GCSI configuration

Almost all communication between GCSI-compliant servers passes through the Hub. The Hub has a number of significant capabilities:
- The Hub maintains connections to servers (parser, speech recognizer, backend, etc.), and routes messages (in the form of frames) among them.
- The Hub can be configured to log aspects of this message traffic.
- The message traffic routing in the Hub can be programmed via a scripting language that controls the flow through each dialog turn. The default scripting language is the MIT scripting language, but users can opt to use no scripting language or incorporate their own. In the MIT scripting language, message traffic is governed by named rule sequences called **Hub programs**.
- The Hub incorporates an internal server named Builtin to implement user-visible administrative tasks, such as establishing breakpoints, redirecting message traffic to other Hub programs, or forcing the Hub to exit.
- The Hub segments its interactions by **session**, which allows multiple users to interact simultaneously with the same configuration of servers. To the greatest degree possible, communication between Hub and servers is transparently session-aware.

The server library provides a number of convenient capabilities for managing the data and communications, including:
– Support for defining **dispatch functions**, which are invoked in response to messages from the Hub, and
– Support for backchannel connections called **brokers** for high-bandwidth data that can be passed directly from server to server.

These tools combine to provide the developer a great deal of flexibility and power in constructing spoken dialog systems.

3.2 Example

As a brief, concrete illustration, consider a small portion of a spoken dialog interaction in a system configured as in *Figure 2*. *Figure 3* shows a new structured message, named `FromAudio`, being sent from the audio server to the Hub. Frames are used to represent these messages; in their printed representation, they're delimited by curly brackets ([2]). The opening bracket is immediately followed by a character indicating the frame type ("c" for "clause" in all the cases in this chapter), then by a white space-delimited frame name, and finally a set of key-value pairs (elided in *Figure 3*).

In *Figure 3*, arrow 1 shows the new message being sent to the hub. The message name `FromAudio` matches the name of a program in the Hub, and as a result the program takes over the message traffic routing. This program contains a rule which instructs the Hub to send a message named `Recognizer.Recognize`.[1] The Hub constructs the message according to the instructions in the rule, and sends it to the speech recognition server, shown in arrow 2. The server looks in its table of dispatch functions for the appropriate dispatch function to invoke when it receives a message named `Recognizer.Recognize`, and invokes the `Recognize` dispatch function as a result.

[1] The programmer configures the Hub with a registry of servers and the messages they support, which is how the Hub chooses the server to receive each message.

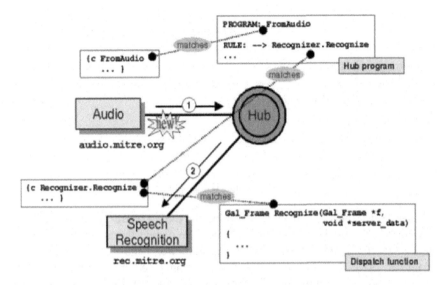

Figure 3. A sample GCSI interaction: from audio to SR

3.3 Hub scripting

The vast majority of the flexibility supported by the GCSI is embodied in the properties of the GCSI Hub, and in particular its scripting capability. A few details will illuminate the discussion below.

When the Hub receives a new message, it does one of three things:

1. If it finds a Hub program whose name matches the name of the new message, it invokes that program. This case is illustrated in *Figure 3* above. This is called a **scripted interaction**.
2. Otherwise, if it finds a server which supports a dispatch function whose name matches the name of the new message, it forwards the message to that server. This is called a **scriptless interaction**.
3. If it finds neither a program or a dispatch function which matches, it discards the message.

In addition to its name, each Hub program consists of a sequence of rules that cause messages to be sent to the connected servers. Each rule indicates the conditions under which the messages are sent, the name of the message to be sent, how to construct the message, and how to digest the result. The Hub memory state which is accessed and updated during this process consists of a set of key-value pairs, and is called a **token**. *Figure 4* illustrates a sample rule:

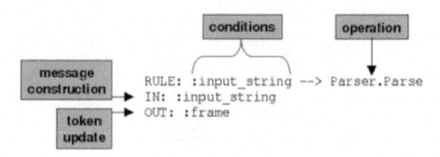

Figure 4. A sample Hub program rule

This rule states that if there's a value for the :input_string key in the token, the Hub should construct a message named Parse and send it to the server named Parser. Furthermore, the value of the :input_string key in the token should be the value of the :input_string key in the message. Finally, if the reply message contains a key named :frame, that key-value pair should be copied into the token.[2]

This is a very simple illustration of the function of Hub programs. As we proceed, we'll see how this basic functionality, and more complex functionality built upon it, helps us achieve our design goals. In the remainder of this chapter, we'll concentrate on those features, in design, implementation and logistics, which are most crucial to realizing the goals outlined in Section 2.2.

4. DESIGN

We begin with the notion of a **service**. A service is an implementation of a conceptual capability such as speech recognition, speech synthesis, or database retrieval. We don't want to specify a list of services needed for dialog systems, because in many cases we frankly don't know. Even when we have a reasonable idea what the services are, we don't know what their boundaries should be, e.g., how much semantic interpretation should be done in the parser or in the dialog module, or which service should handle reference resolution. We expect that as the user community experiments with the different possibilities, the best practice will emerge; so our ideal

---

[2] You can also copy these values from one key in the source token or message to a different key in the target token or message. See Section 4.2.2 below.

infrastructure ought to say a lot about how to construct a service, but nothing about what individual services should do.

In order to construct a service, we require three things:

1. A set of datatypes (certainly simple types, but possibly complex ones as well)
2. A set of operations on those datatypes (which, together with the datatypes, could be object-oriented), for which names and valences must be determined
3. A communications layer over which the service is accessed, an invocation strategy (synchronous vs. asynchronous, for example) for the service, and a topology for how services are connected (e.g., hub and spoke vs. peer-to-peer)

While we need to provide tools to address all three of these dimensions, we also want to limit as little as possible which choices along these dimensions are made. So, for instance, the ideal infrastructure would support both synchronous and asynchronous invocation. Furthermore, in order to encourage the emergence of standards and "best practice", the ideal infrastructure would allow members of the community to combine conflicting choices in a single system, and move between conflicting choices easily (e.g., make use of multiple speech recognizers, one designed according to a synchronous paradigm and another according to an asynchronous paradigm). Finally, the ideal infrastructure will allow community members to accomplish this negotiation **without modifying the services themselves**. In the sections to follow, we'll consider each of these three dimensions and show first how the GCSI enables a wide array of choices, and then how the GCSI enables negotiating conflicting choices.

4.1 Datatypes

4.1.1 Datatype flexibility

The GCSI supports a fairly rich set of basic datatypes: strings, integers, floats, heterogeneous lists of elements of any datatype, arrays of integers and floats of various sizes, and finally, frames. Frames can be used to construct complex datatypes of your choosing. For instance, *Figure 5* shows a frame which might implement a structure which represents the result of querying a database. The frame name can be used to indicate the structure's type, and the key-value pairs the slots and values in the structure.

```
{c DBResult
   :columns ( "fltno" "airline" )
```

```
:tuples (( 576 "TWA" )
         ( 1408 "AA" )) }
```

Figure 5. A frame implementing a complex datatype

Unlike CORBA, for instance, the GCSI doesn't support the declaration of new datatypes. This has some notable shortcomings; for example, automatic datatype checking is lost, and you can't implement any sort of object-oriented inheritance based on object type. However, there is one absolutely crucial advantage: by fixing the set of datatypes, we ensure that the central Hub doesn't need to know anything about the datatypes of the various servers it communicates with. In a heterogeneous distributed environment, one where service standards haven't been established yet, this is an indispensable benefit.

4.1.2 Datatype conflicts

So what if servers which share the same conceptual datatypes differ in the details of the implementation of these types? In Section 2.3, we described one such situation, where one synthesizer treats capitalized text as words and another treats it as acronyms. A language generator which interacts with these synthesizers needs to be aware of the difference. Similarly, we've also encountered cases where one database module returns a set of tuples whose values are already interpreted as integers, floats or strings, as illustrated in *Figure 5*, while another returns tuples all of whose values are strings.

In cases like these, the appropriate solution is to introduce a small server to do the data transformation. This may appear to be an overly onerous process, but in fact, it is not; in general, building and adding a server is extremely simple. In most cases, it turns out to be far preferable to modifying either of the servers involved, and the additional server, in most cases, does not add any visible processing overhead to the system as a whole. Because the Hub scripting language manages the flow of control, it allows the programmer to insert the new data transformation server at the appropriate execution point, in between the two incompatible servers.

4.2 Operation names and valences

4.2.1 Name and valence flexibility

When the GCSI Hub sends a message to a server, the server maps the name of the message to an appropriate function to invoke, which we call a

dispatch function. The frame that the Hub has constructed as a message is passed to that function, which extracts the appropriate values from the set of key-value pairs, checks their types, performs the appropriate operations, constructs the appropriate reply message, and returns it.

One obvious question to ask is: why key-value pairs? There's nothing in the Hub scripting language that is incompatible with passing the values specified in the IN: line as a sequence, rather than a set of key-value pairs. We believe that there are a number of reasons to prefer key-value pairs.

First, it vastly simplifies the process of dispatch function registration in the server, because every dispatch function has exactly the same function signature. We don't have to worry about functions with three arguments vs. functions with five, and how they need to be handled differently. Especially in compiled languages (like C) and in languages which don't have sequences as a basic datatype (again, like C) to use for argument lists, it eliminates a range of headaches.

Second, it means that there's a common way of implementing the entire range of argument types found in programming languages like Python and Allegro Common Lisp: required arguments, optional arguments, and arguments passed as key-value pairs. The key-value representation is the most general, and represents a very small overhead over ordered arguments.

Third, it's now possible for multiple sets of key-value pairs to "inhabit" the same invocation, if you so desire. For instance, let's say you're using one of two parsers, and you don't care which one. One pays attention to the :input_string key, and another pays attention to the :string key. You can set up your Hub script to try to pass both keys; if only one is found, only one will be passed, but if both are found, whichever server you happen to be using will pay attention to the key it's interested in and ignore the other.

Fourth, returning a set of key-value pairs makes multiple value returns transparent. Many programming languages don't even have this capability (again, like C), and resort to various tricks to get around this limitation, such as building structures to pass around or various kinds of pointer manipulation. Using key-value pairs gives us a programming-language-independent model of how dispatch functions consume and provide data.

Finally, it's worth noting that there is no provision in the GCSI to enforce datatype restrictions on the key-value pairs themselves. That is, while it's possible for the developer to declare the datatypes of various keys when the service is constructed, the infrastructure will not automatically generate an error if a datatype mismatch is encountered at run-time. Providing an option for this sort of enforcement is one way the GCSI could be improved.

4.2.2 Name and valence conflicts

The Hub scripting language allows us to handle the range of mismatch possibilities for operation names and valences. We encountered this problem when switching between recognizers and synthesizers in the system we outlined in Section 2.3, but those cases are complicated by other issues as well. So let's look at a simple case: the recognizer server wants to cause a string to be parsed, but it believes the operation in question is named Parse, while the server which actually provides the service has an operation named ParseSentence. The scripting language handles this by fielding the incoming Parse message, and routing it to the ParseSentence operation:

```
PROGRAM: Parse

RULE: :input_string —> ParseSentence
IN: :input_string
...
```

Figure 6. Resolving an operation name mismatch

If the originating server expects a reply, the Hub will return the token state to the originating server when the program concludes; otherwise, the Hub discards the token state. In this way, the behavior of the remote service is transparent to the originating server, even if the operation names don't match.

A somewhat more interesting case arises when the valences don't match, e.g., the key names the invoked server expects differ from the key names the invoking server provides. The Hub scripting language provides a mapping facility in the IN: and OUT: lines of Hub program rules which allows the programmer to map key names from the token into different key names in the message being sent, and vice versa upon return. In more complex cases, the keys don't merely fail to match, but also represent multiple values which must be combined into a single value, or single values which must be split up (e.g., if a database server returns a result in a single frame as in *Figure 5,* but the caller expects to see the columns and tuples as separate top-level keys). In these cases, the technique described here can be combined with inserting simple servers as illustrated in Section 4.1.2.

4.3 Invocation and topology

4.3.1 Hub and spoke vs. peer to peer

The GCSI, like OAA [5], TRINDI [6], TRIPS [2], and the SIRIDUS recommendation [13], is fundamentally a hub-and-spoke architecture. That is, information flows from module to module through a central routing facility (the Hub) rather than directly from module to module. For instance, in a peer-to-peer model, the sample configuration in *Figure 2* might look like this:

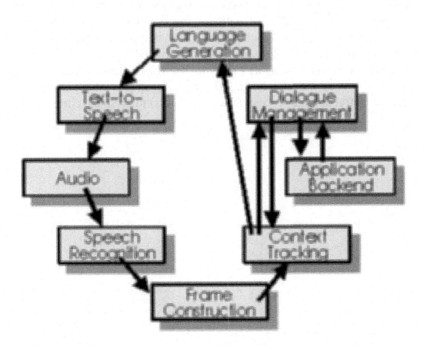

Figure 7. Peer-to-peer configuration

Although communication in this configuration is more direct, we'll see in a moment that the hub-and-spoke configuration is vastly more flexible, and in fact crucial to our needs. While it is absolutely possible for one server to contact another directly and communicate with it via structured messages, we do not make use of this mechanism in normal circumstances. In fact, we will see that all the significant invocation strategies we wish to explore can be modeled fairly transparently on top of a hub-and-spoke configuration.[3]

4.3.2 Invocation and topology flexibility

Although the physical configuration of GCSI-compliant systems is hub-and-spoke, this is actually a source of flexibility which allows us to model the range of possible invocation strategies and topologies.

Let's start with the distinction between synchronous and asynchronous invocation. When the Hub invokes a dispatch function, this boils down to whether the dispatch function continues the flow of control by returning a result to the caller (which we will call the **synchronous** strategy), or by issuing a new message (which we will call the **asynchronous** strategy). *Figure 8* illustrates a recognizer which is instructed to recognize audio, and returns the recognized string as a reply for the Hub to decide what to do with next. *Figure 9,* on the other hand, illustrates a recognizer which issues a new message instructing the receiver (the Hub, that is) to parse the corresponding string.

---

[3] For a discussion of the implementational efficiency of such a configuration, see Section 5.3.

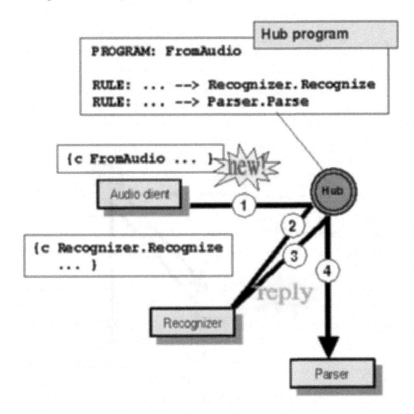

Figure 8. Synchronous interaction

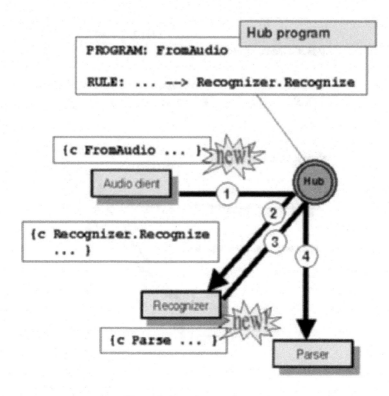

Figure 9. Asynchronous interaction

These two invocation strategies correspond to two different topologies, and implicitly to two different philosophies about how distributed systems work. When we think of services as synchronous, we envision a configuration in which a central controller determines when each service will be invoked, and makes decisions about what to do next based on the results of that invocation. This model corresponds to a hub-and-spoke configuration. On the other hand, when we think of services as asynchronous, we envision a configuration where each service makes its own decision about how to proceed. There is no central controller in this model, and the most compatible logical topology is peer-to-peer. Both of these philosophies have been exploited in dialog systems ([11] vs. [2], for instance) and both must be supported.

The support for the synchronous, hub-and-spoke, central control case is straightforward; it corresponds directly to the physical hub-and-spoke topology, and involves synchronous calls to servers as illustrated in *Figure*

8[4]. The support for the decentralized peer-to-peer typology requires some further clarification. Recall from Section 3.3 that when the Hub receives a new message, it either invokes a matching program or forwards the message to a qualified server. In the latter case (the scriptless interaction), the Hub is acting as no more than a communications channel, and conceptually the control is decentralized and peer-to-peer (albeit with an intervening "hop" through the Hub). Indeed, the TRIPS infrastructure [2] exploits exactly this tension between logical and physical topologies.

Finally, and just as significantly, the choice to seize control of a new message or pass it on is made by the Hub on a message-by-message basis. So the Hub supports not only both the strategies described here, but also a mix of these strategies.

4.3.3 Invocation conflicts

It's not just the Hub which has the option of sending synchronous or asynchronous messages; the new messages which the servers send to the Hub can be synchronous or asynchronous as well. In these cases, the Hub really has no choice but to respect the expectations of the sending server, because the server won't function properly otherwise. If that server expects a response but receives a new message instead, it will still wait forever for the response, and if the server expects a new message but receives a response instead, it will ignore the response and fail to continue the interaction.

In order to respect the expectations of the sending server, the Hub may have to resolve invocation conflicts. In order to see this, let's consider a simple interaction where a dialog manager sends a message (via the Hub) to a database in order to retrieve information to provide to the user. This interaction involves four messages, numbered in order in *Figure 10:*

---

[4] The synchronous model usually isn't pure; in general a configuration of GCSI Hub and servers will remain quiescent until some server initiates an activity (e.g., audio available on a microphone). In other words, in GCSI the initial message is typically asynchronous, and in fact there's currently no facility for the Hub to poll input devices (since there's no explicit loop facility in the Hub scripting language, nor are there sufficiently fine-grained timer-based events).

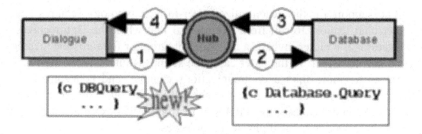

Figure 10. Dialog module consults database

In this context, let's consider two dialog servers and two database servers. Dialog server A expects a synchronous interaction; it sends a message to the Hub and waits for a reply containing the database information. Dialog server B expects an asynchronous interaction; it sends a message to the Hub and expects a new message containing the database information. Both of these designs are reasonable and plausible. Similarly, when database server A receives a request for information from the Hub, it provides the information as a reply, while database server B provides the information in a new message.

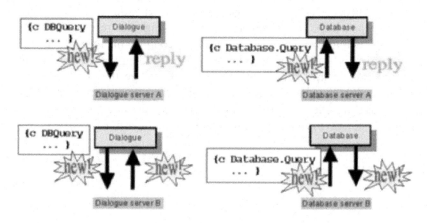

Figure 11. Dialog and backend, synchronous and asynchronous

Dialog server A and database server A do not conflict; the Hub receives a new message from dialog server A and relays it to database server A, and relays the reply back to the dialog server. Similarly, dialog server B and database server B do not conflict; the Hub relays the new message from dialog server B to database server B, and relays the resulting new message from database server B to dialog server B. The problem arises when we have to pair dialog server A with database server B, or vice versa.

We first consider pairing dialog server B (asynchronous) with database server A (synchronous). This case is trivial. The Hub takes control of the incoming DBQuery message, and sends the appropriate message to the backend server. When the reply comes in, the Hub sends a new message to the dialog server, which the Hub does not wait for a response to:

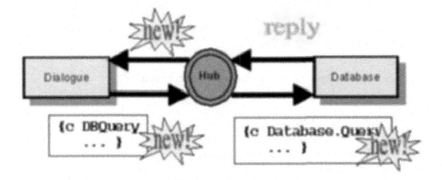

Figure 12. Asynchronous caller, synchronous callee

```
PROGRAM: DBQuery

RULE: … —> Database.Query
IN: :query
OUT: :columns :tuples

RULE: :columns —> Dialog.DBResult
IN: :columns :tuples
OUT: none!
```

Figure 13. Program for synchronous caller, synchronous callee

The pairing of dialog server A (synchronous) with database server B (asynchronous) is only slightly more complex. In this case, the Hub takes control of the incoming DBQuery message, as before, and sends the appropriate message to the backend server. However, in this case, we insert the CONTINUE_REPLY: directive in the rule, which instructs the Hub to wait for a new message of a particular form and treat it as a reply. Once the program ends, the Hub returns the token state to the calling server (the dialog server, that is).

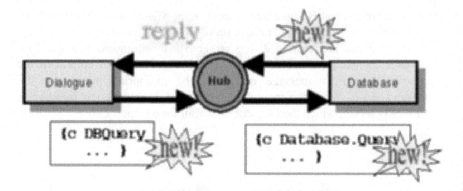

Figure 14. Synchronous caller, asynchronous callee

```
PROGRAM: DBQuery

RULE: ... -> Database.Query
IN: :query
CONTINUE_REPLY: {c DBResult }
OUT: :columns :tuples
```

Figure 15. Program for synchronous caller, asynchronous callee

So again, we see that the GCSI not only models alternative strategies, but also reconciles conflicts between them.

4.4   Heterogeneous run-time situations

These sorts of mismatches may not be determined in advance. The memory states in the Hub (which include the token state we discussed in Section 3.3, as well as a global memory state and a state associated with each session) can be updated and accessed by the Hub scripting language to modify the message flow in real time. For instance, it's simple to modify the Hub memory state to switch among recognizers or synthesizers based on GUI feedback or server-provided information (e.g., what language the speaker is speaking). In these cases, it's straightforward to use the Hub scripting capabilities to encapsulate and compensate for the sorts of contrasting assumptions we've discussed here.

5. IMPLEMENTATION AND LOGISTICS

At this point, we've illustrated the enormous range of possibilities that the GCSI enables, and how it can negotiate among them at runtime. Using these tools, individual sites are free to model their services however they choose, and still be able to share their services with other sites and to incorporate services from other sites into their own end-to-end systems. However, meeting our design considerations would be pointless if the GCSI presented implementational or logistical obstacles to obtaining, installing, learning, or using it.

In some sense, ensuring a broad enough base of users to generate a representative array of alternative approaches means thinking about the GCSI in terms of "market share". These considerations, in many cases, having nothing to do with the functional capabilities of the software in question, and everything to do with the so-called "human factors" of software consumption. In this Section, we describe how the GCSI addresses some of these issues. For related discussion, see [12].

5.1 Obtaining and installing the GCSI

The GCSI software and documentation are available for download at http://communicator.sourceforge.net. They are distributed under a very liberal open source license. We believe that the cleanest and least onerous licensing and distribution model for software like the GCSI is an open source model. With the appropriate open source licensing properties, there are no barriers to freely distributing and redistributing the GCSI, or to distributing dialog systems created using the GCSI, or to building commercial products based on it. Obtaining such software involves neither signatures nor financial resources, and it is thus available to the broadest possible audience for the least possible effort and expense.

Once a potential user obtains the software, it's important that s/he find it simple and straightforward to install. The GCSI is clear and well-documented; the system is supported on Windows NT, Intel Linux, and Sparc Solaris, is known to work on a number of others, and can be easily ported to new platforms.

5.2 Learning the GCSI

Once the software is installed, the user should find a straightforward path to learning it. The GCSI provides a step-by-step introduction and tutorial [14] complete with exercises, which the user can work through at his or her own pace. In addition, the GCSI is distributed with extensive examples, as well as a toy end-to-end dialog system which illustrates one possible configuration of GCSI-compliant servers. All the elements of the GCSI – Hub, servers, examples – are extensively documented, both in HTML and PDF formats.

5.3   Efficiency

The GCSI is relatively efficient both in terms of space and time. The GCSI server wrapper adds approximately 2 MB to the size of a given executable. On a 333 Mhz UltraSparc running Solaris 2.7, the throughput of a simple server which echoes messages is on the order of 1200 to 1400 messages per second for messages of a typical size. A Hub intervening between a client and this server can process approximately 500 messages per second.[5] These speeds are much more than fast enough to support coarse- or medium-granularity interaction between servers, where the number of messages associated with a single user utterance numbers in the dozens at most in current implementations.[6]

5.4   Integrating the GCSI with other software packages

The GCSI server library is based on a straightforward event-based programming model. This model provides maximum implementational flexibility by enforcing an encapsulation of all the important behaviors in the GCSI, as well as providing hooks for invoking them in response to externally-defined events like finding data available on a socket, or the expiration of a timer. The GCSI exploits this model in four ways.

First, the GCSI comes with its own event loop, which manages the registration of these events and their associated behaviors. In the default situation, this is the way GCSI-compliant servers are implemented.

Second, the GCSI makes public the hooks it provides for registering GCSI events, so that developers can add other timer- or socket-based events

---

[5] These speeds do not translate into equivalent speeds on the client side, due to the properties of the top-level processing loops in the Hub and server. With a single client, the Hub or server spends approximately half its time sleeping, and as a result, the speeds for a single client are approximately 600 to 700 round trips in the direct case and approximately 250 round trips with a Hub intervening. However, two clients saturate the top-level processing loops, and can be handled as quickly as one, from which we derive the throughput numbers for the Hub and server. For more than two clients, the performance degrades as expected.

[6] We have not experimented with using this infrastructure for fine-grained interactions, such as a parser looking up lexical entries in a remote dictionary via the Hub. For certain sizes and volumes of messages, you may encounter delays.

to a default GCSI-compliant server, such as a poll on an audio channel or typed console input.

Third, the event-based model allows the GCSI to be embedded in other event loops, such as those provided by windowing systems like Tcl/Tk and Motif or by other event-loop-based software like CORBA implementations. This means that there's a clear path to building GCSI-enabled GUI applications, or to constructing software bridges between GCSI Hubs and other distributed processing tools.

Finally, the event-based model means that it's simple to use the core C library as the basis for GCSI-compliant server libraries in other programming languages, and use native facilities for scheduling the GCSI events. The GCSI is distributed with programming language bindings for Java, Python and Allegro Common Lisp, the last two of which exploit this feature of the core C library.

As with the range of available platforms, in the best of all possible circumstances, the GCSI would be delivered with a far wider range of programming language bindings; however, resource limitations have made this sort of generalization impossible.

5.5   The Open Source Toolkit

Finally, as part of its efforts to build a community of users, MITRE has coordinated the development of an open source toolkit of dialog system components. These components include wrappers for readily available open source software such as CMU's Sphinx recognizer and Festival synthesizer and the PostGres relational database system. These components also include full servers such as desktop and telephone audio components. Some of these wrappers and servers have been contributed by MITRE, others by the developers of the servers themselves. We anticipate that as our community of users grows, the range of available GCSI-compliant software will also grow, helping us to achieve our goal of information exchange and exploration of standards and "best practice".

6.   STANDARDS, COMMERCIALIZATION AND THE GCSI

Let's assume, for the moment, that the GCSI succeeds in building the sort of community we're describing. What steps must we then take to leverage this community for standardization, and ultimately commercial uses?

6.1   Standardization in spoken dialog

The history of standardization efforts in the area of spoken dialog is rather short. It covers the following efforts:
- The Discourse Research Initiative has proposed the DAMSL tag set [15], a proposed research standard for dialog annotation.
- The SAPI [16] and JSAPI [17] specifications are industry proposals for C++- and Java-specific APIs for speech recognition and synthesis.
- The W3C Voice Browsers committee [3] hosted by the World Wide Web Consortium, is an international standards effort which has issued draft specifications for dialog, speech recognition rewrite and N-gram grammars, speech synthesis markup, and semantic interpretation. On March 16, 2004, the speech recognition and dialog proposals were endorsed as official W3C Recommendations.
- The VoiceXML Forum [18] is an industry consortium which produced VoiceXML 1.0, a synthesis of a number of previous dialog markup languages and the basis of the W3CVB dialog proposal.
- The SALT Forum [19] is an industry consortium which is developing a specification to speech-enable existing Web pages. The SALT 1.0 specification was submitted to the W3C for consideration on July 31, 2002. In other words, although there's been a great deal of standards activity, the process has only recently started to yield consensus."

We should not be surprised by this situation. Speech and spoken dialog have only recently emerged from the laboratory, and well-thought-out standards trail their inspiring implementations by a good margin. For example, the W3C Voice Browsers draft specification for speech synthesis markup, which one of the most mature of the W3CVB drafts, is based on the JSML speech synthesis markup language [20]. Efforts such as JSML have been underway since 1997 at the latest, and have yielded a number of working implementations, one of which is available for the open-source Festival speech synthesizer. In spite of this broad community effort, more than four years later, no international standard has been approved.

6.2   Existing standards proposals and the GCSI

Does the GCSI support the proposed run-time standards listed here? Not really. But it's important to note that these run-time standards are still evolving, and attempting to track them implementationally would be a waste of valuable research dollars. Furthermore, in many ways, asking about support is the wrong question. The emerging run-time standards address a number of dimensions of spoken dialog, including the input, output and configuration of the components, their APIs, and the communications layer which connects them. In all these dimensions, compatibility, rather than support, is the key. Let's consider these dimensions in turn.

First, let's consider the input, output and configuration of the components, i.e., the data standards. The GCSI says nothing about these at all. We noted above, for instance, that the Festival speech synthesizer can support JSML. We provide a GCSI-compliant wrapper for Festival in the Open Source Toolkit described in Section 5.5, and the wrapper is fully capable of sending marked-up text input to the Festival engine to be synthesized. As long as the datatypes are supported by the GCSI (or can be represented in a supported datatype; see Section 4.1), these data standards are orthogonal to the concerns of the GCSI, and in most cases completely transparent.

The case of API standards is somewhat different. The GCSI is designed specifically to be able to explore different forms of these APIs (see Section 4.2). However, this flexibility is in no way incompatible with existing proposed APIs such as SAPI and JSAPI. In fact, the Open Source Toolkit includes sample GCSI-compliant middleware which is intended to wrap around a JSAPI-compliant speech engine, and has been shown to work with IBM's ViaVoice. Furthermore, as the message sets for GCSI-compliant modules converge over time, they can easily be translated into programming-language-specific fixed APIs, or programming-language-independent service definitions in terms of, e.g., CORBA IDL.

The GCSI communications layer is the only one of these dimensions which could realistically be said to be incompatible. However, the GCSI framework was never intended to be a basis for proposed standards; it's a platform for exploration of possible approaches which is more flexible and reconfigurable than likely standards platforms. It's far more important for the GCSI to be easily translatable into a form which assumes a standard communications layer (as in the case of CORBA IDL described immediately above). In addition, it should hardly be surprising that the GCSI isn't going to be a dialog system standard; it's designed to inspire standards, and standards almost always differ from their inspiring implementations.

6.3 Moving forward

It should now be clear that if we succeed in building our community, we have an opportunity to have a clear impact on the standards process, by virtue of the flexibility and compatibility of the GCSI. In this final section, we present a few concrete ways to exploit that opportunity.

First, the GCSI is a platform for disseminating the expertise which leads to implementations which inspire standards. For instance, the ability of the user to interrupt the system's spoken output (i.e., barge-in) is a fairly new option. However, the implications of this option have not been deeply explored. One issue which systems must confront is deciding whether to recognize the user's contribution as an interrupt (e.g., "shut up", or stop talking) or a backchannel acknowledgement (e.g., "uh huh", or keep talking). Another issue is determining the relationship between how much audio was successfully presented and how much information was successfully presented; knowing that half the audio was presented doesn't help the system determine how much information was presented, or what portion of the information. In an advanced dialog system, addressing these issues correctly can mean the difference between a satisfied user and one who vows never to use the system again. If we address these issues in the context of modules which are GCSI-compliant, it's easy for other sites to test these hypotheses and compare their own alternatives.

Second, GCSI-compliant systems can serve as reference implementations for ideas which are already making their way into proposed standards. For example, the W3CVB dialog markup specification includes an algorithm for template filling which can operate opportunistically; that is, it will recognize slot fills presented by the user which are still needed but it did not prompt for. This sort of capability is fairly new, and may not yet be mature. The experiences of developers of GCSI-compliant systems may be able to inform decisions about dimensions of emerging specifications such as this.

Finally, GCSI-compliant systems can be used as operational prototypes, e.g. to test new functionality with early adopters, even before standards-compliant systems can be built. A number of GCSI-compliant components, such as Festival and the open-source Sphinx recognizer, are quite capable tools, and the GCSI can help provide access to the most recent research results represented in these tools. And while in general, the GCSI may be too complex and flexible for an actual commercial deployment, there are no legal impediments to doing just that.

7.   CONCLUSION

Establishing standards is exceptionally difficult and time-consuming work. Under such circumstances, it's important to ensure that there is a path for developing, testing, and discussing possible standards directions, if possible even as research progresses. Through its flexible structure and its attention to the "human factors" of software consumption, the GCSI is ideally situated to foster the emergence of the appropriate community of users. In addition to the DARPA Communicator program, two other dialog research programs have recently adopted the GCSI: AMITIES [21, 22] and

MUST. We hope that the momentum provided by the GCSI and the open source toolkit will make a long-term contribution to the advancement in the state of the art in dialog system design.

REFERENCES

[1] H. Cunningham, "Software Architecture for Language Engineering." Sheffield, England: University of Sheffield, 2000.

[2] J. Allen, D. Byron, M. Dzikovksa, G. Ferguson, L. Galescu, and A. Stent, "Towards a generic dialog shell," *Natural Language Engineering*, vol. 6, pp. 213-228, 2000.

[3] W3C, "W3C Voice Browser Group Home Page", http://www.w3.org/Voice/,

[4] "Communicator [Web site]", http://www.darpa.mil/ipto/research/com/index.html., 2002.

[5] D. L. Martin, A. J. Cheyer, and D. B. Moran, "The open agent architecture: A framework for building distributed software systems," *Applied Artificial Intelligence*, vol. 13, pp. 91-128, 1999.

[6] S. Larsson, P. Bohlin, J. Bos, and D. Traum, "TRINDIKIT 1.0 Manual," 1999.

[7] A. Aaron, "Speech Recognition for DARPA Communicator," presented at Proceedings of ICASSP 2001, Salt Lake City, Utah, USA, 2001.

[8] E. Levin, S. Narayanan, R. Pieraccini, K. Biatov, E. Boccherini, W. Di Fabbrizio, S. L. Eckert, M. Pokrovsky, P. Rahim, P. Ruscitti, and M. Walker, "The AT&T DARPA communicator mixed initiative spoken dialog system," presented at Proceedings of ICSLP 2000, Beijing, PRC, 2000.

[9] B. Pellom, W. Ward, and S. Pradhan, "The CU Communicator: An architecture for dialog systems," presented at Proceedings of ICSLP-2000, Beijing, PRC, 2000.

[10] D. Stallard, "Talk'n'Travel: A conversational system for air travel planning," presented at Proceedings of the Association for Computational Linguistics 6th Applied Natural Language Processing Conference (ANLP-2000), Seattle, WA, USA, 2000.

[11] V. Zue, S. Seneff, J. Glass, J. Polifroni, C. Pao, T. J. Hazen, and L. Hetherington, "Jupiter: A Telephone-Based Conversational Interface for Weather Information," *IEEE Transactions on Speech and Audio Processing*, vol. 8, 2000.

[12] S. Bayer and e. al., "Dialog interaction with the DARPA Communicator: The development of useful software," presented at Proceedings of HLT 2001, San Diego, CA, USA, 2001.

[13] I. Lewin, C. J. Rupp, J. Hieronymus, D. Milwards, S. Larrson, and A. Berman, "Siridus system architecture and interface report (baseline)," EU Fifth Framework Information Society Technologies SIRIDUS (Specification, Interaction and Reconfiguration in dialog understanding systems) project IST-1999-10516 Deliverable D6.1, July 2000.

[14] "Galaxy Communicator documentation: Toplevel Index", http://communicator.sourceforge.net/sites/MITRE/distributions/GalaxyCommunicator/docs/manual/index.html, January 2002-May 30 2003.

[15] M. Core and J. Allen, "Coding Dialogs with the DAMSL Annotation Scheme," presented at AAAI Fall Symposium on Communicative Action in Humans and Machines, Boston, MA, USA, 1997.

[16] Microsoft, "Speech.NET", http://www.microsoft.com/speech/, 2003.

[17] "Java™ Speech API [Web site]", http://java.sun.com/products/java-media/speech/, 1995-2002.

[18] VoiceXML Forum, http://www.voicexmlforum.org,

[19]   "Salt Forum", http://www.saltforum.org, 2002.
[20]   "Java™ Speech API Markup Language Specification, Version 0.6", http://java.sun.com/products/java-media/speech/forDevelopers/JSML/index.html, October, 1999-May 2002.
[21]   "Automated Multilingual Interaction with Information and Services", http://www.dcs.shef.ac.uk/nlp/amities/. 2001-2002 May 30.
[22]   "MUST - MUltimodal, multilingual information services for small mobile terminals", http://www.eurescom.de/public/projects/P1100-series/p1104/default.asp,

Chapter 10

Building Spoken-Language Collaborative Interface Agents

Candace L. Sidner
Mitsubishi Electric Research Laboratories

Key words: collaboration, conversation, interfaces, collaborative interface agents, spoken
dialog, subset languages

Abstract: This article reports on experiences with collaborative interface agents that use
spoken dialog to collaborate with users manipulating graphical user interface
applications. Collaborative interface agents provide users significant new
capabilities: ways to manage tasks while leaving many of the details to the
agent. The article presents four different collaborative agents and associated
applications. It reports on lessons learned in building these agents, including
the importance of choosing tasks that can relieve the user of unnecessary
detail, and providing speech capabilities that are useable for a wide range of
users. In particular, the article reports on the success in developing a subset
language for speech understanding in one of the agents. Finally, the article
discusses the advantages of using the explanation capabilities in collaborative
agents to help users learn new interface functionality

1. INTRODUCTION

This article reports on experiences with collaborative interface agents
that use spoken dialog to collaborate with users who are manipulating
graphical user interface (GUI) applications. A team of researchers and
software engineers[1] spanning two commercial research organizations (Lotus
Development Corporation and Mitsubishi Electric Research Laboratories)

---

[1] The systems reported here resulted from the efforts over time of several people in
addition to the author. Thanks to: Carolyn Boettner, Clifton Forlines, Bret Harsham, David
McDonald, Chris Maloof, Neal Lesh, Charles Rich, Bent Schmidt-Nielsen and Peter Wolf.

built four such agents. This article reports on our original goals in building spoken-language collaborative interface agents, on our experience in developing agents for four different applications, and on the lessons we have learned throughout this exploratory process. As this article will make clear, many current GUIs do not easily lend themselves to adding a collaborative agent, so using a collaborative agent challenges developers to define the agent's tasks so that they will reduce the user's interface burden.

Our goals have evolved over the several years during which these four agents were built. The original goal was to understand how interacting with a collaborative agent would differ from just giving commands to an interface. As the work progressed, we began to focus more on making use of the powerful capabilities of software agents in reducing the user's burden in using complex applications. We also found that the speech recognition technology needed to be better utilized to make the recognition highly reliable for every user without extensive voice data collection for the recognizer. Finally, we experimented with agents that provided explanations for how to achieve tasks using the interface. We pursued these goals with four collaborative interface agents and associated applications that are discussed in this paper.

Effective collaboration between a person and an interface agent depends fundamentally upon the agent being able to hold a conversation about the purposes of the collaboration. Computational linguistics research on conversation [1] has identified several key components to such conversations:

- the role of segmentation in determining the major units of a conversation,
- the relation between the intentions of the conversational participants to the purposes conveyed in conversation,
- mechanisms for change in the participants' purposes during the conversation,
- and the focus of attention, that is, the relative salience of purposes, objects, actions and other entities as the conversation unfolds.

Combining these aspects of conversation with collaboration requires relating the intentions conveyed in utterances to the tasks of the collaboration. The collaborative interface agents discussed in this article use these aspects of conversation and the capacity to collaborate in practical interface applications. These agents collaborate with users in tasks for email, scheduling meetings and two versions of TV entertainment control.

One of the lessons learned in building collaborative interface agents, namely, to provide speech understanding that is feasible with today's technology, has been incorporated into the later interfaces reported on here. The first two agents, for collaboration on email and for scheduling meetings, understood only some of the utterances users typically would say to them.

Without an extensive data collection effort, we found that not every user could talk to these agents because we only predicted a portion of the vocabulary and grammar that users spoke with. Unless every user could easily talk to the agent, the systems built were an insightful view of the future, but not very practical for the average user now. To make collaborative agents usable now required a focus on making speech intelligible for the agent. The fourth agent, for navigation of TV schedules and program recording tasks, constrains how the user can speak but does so with persistently present information about the legal utterances the user can say. The resulting conversations are direct and practical, but lack the brevity typical in conversations among people. Improving the naturalness of these conversations depends upon not only more powerful speech recognition technology, but also many other capabilities, such as better turn taking, observation the conversational partner, interpretation of gesture, and more knowledge of the implicit aspects of the domain.

A second lesson learned concerns the benefits of collaboration. Collaboration has the power to transform the user from a low level clerk seeing to every detail of his tasks into a manager of his tasks, who delegates details to an agent. Collaborative agents are most beneficial when the agent is given sub-tasks to perform rather than individual GUI acts. Simply replacing pointing at a menu with spoken commands ("File, Open") does not yield useful collaborations for several reasons. First, many GUIs have been designed to optimize the use of the mouse. Speech command of GUI actions is generally no faster than clicking and can be slower when correction for speech errors is included. Even for those actions (for example, search commands) that are faster with speech than the mouse, collaboration does not have enough overall payoff due to the small efficiency gained with speech. Second, the GUI requires users to control every interface action and all the associated tasks. In contrast, we have designed collaborative agents who understand speech and the user's task well enough to do parts of it without detailed supervision. These agents offer even more powerful benefits to users than the point-and-click, manage-every-detail style interfaces users live with now.

2. COLLABORATIVE INTERFACE AGENTS

In order to understand how to use a collaborative interface agent with existing applications, several questions must first be addressed: What exactly is a collaboration? What is a collaborative interface agent? How are collaborative agents different from other systems that have conversations with users?

Collaboration is a process in which two or more participants coordinate their actions toward achieving shared goals [2, 3]. Collaboration between two people who are co-present involves:
- communication between them;
- interaction with the shared artifact that is the locus of their shared goals (e.g., when painting a house, the house is a shared artifact, when trouble shooting a problem under the hood of the car, the engine is the shared artifact);
- and observation of what the other person is doing with the shared artifact.

As the collaboration unfolds, the participants also come to share certain beliefs. Specifically, they come to share beliefs about their intentions to do actions, beliefs about how those actions support their shared goals, beliefs about how to advance the collaboration, and beliefs about the artifacts.

A collaborative interface agent is designed to take the place of one of the human participants in a collaboration involving a shared interface to a computer application [4]. The agent therefore must be able to communicate with the human user, manipulate the interface, and observe the user's manipulation of the interface. It must also be able to come to have shared beliefs of the same type as in the human-human collaboration [2, 3, 5]. A diagram of collaboration between a user and a collaborative interface agent is shown in Figure 1.

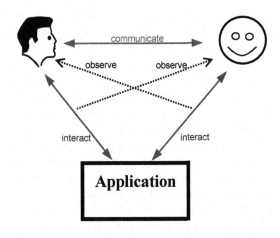

Figure 1. Human-Agent Collaboration

In this article we will focus on collaborative interface agents that communicate via spoken dialog with a user who is using a software application as the shared artifact. Such an agent speaks utterances to a user and understands the user's spoken utterances. Spoken (as opposed to textual) communication is especially valuable when the user's hands and eyes are engaged with the application interface.

2.1 Collaborative Conversations versus Imperative Interactions

While speaking to an interface can be easily argued for, one might wonder why a **collaborative** agent is needed. Why not just replace GUI operations with spoken commands? Our answer largely concerns how to reduce the burden of what users must convey to computers. The imperative command approach treats the computer as a kind of slave to the user's request. It puts the entire burden for managing the overall task on the user so that the user must tell the system exactly what to do at each step.

The imperative command approach suffers from a significant conceptual flaw. Users want to know and say less about the details of applications than they currently do. The mantra of users should be: do more with less input.

Instead, in current GUIs, the user cannot leave out any action, and furthermore, all of the actions are low-level and detailed. Providing GUI commands in speech rather than by pointing and clicking does not address this problem.

Collaboration offers the user something new: a means to be freed from having to even think about portions of his or her tasks. The user describes an action or outcome to the agent, and then the agent undertakes to accomplish the part of the outcome that it knows how to do. The action might take the agent several sub-actions to accomplish, but the user will be freed from performing or even supervising those actions. In accomplishing its sub-tasks, the agent is responsible for asking for the information it lacks when accomplishing its task. However, for this describe-and-act paradigm to work, the agent needs to have a larger context for interpreting what the user is undertaking. The larger context is essential for choosing actions and objects. Collaborative agents are built to have knowledge of the overall task and how all the actions fit together to achieve the entire task.

In the collaboration framework, the agent is not a slave, but functions as a somewhat knowledgeable assistant. It cannot do everything a user can do because it still is not as sophisticated as a human, either in its ability to do tasks in the world, in its understanding users' beliefs and intentions, or in making everyday inferences about the world. It can, however, undertake portions of a user's task and accomplish those actions in light of the user's goals and the known means of achieving them.

Interfaces to applications do not offer such help because they cannot. The interface has extremely little information about what the user is doing. In most existing computer applications, the information that the interface or the application itself does have is generally not used to reason about what the user is doing or wants to achieve. While inroads in certain applications are being made in this direction (for example, the Microsoft paper clip models user activities with Bayesian networks), such software additions do not converse with the user about the user's goals or means of achieving those goals. So at best, the interface "agent" guesses what is going on. Our approach relies on using the human-human collaboration model more closely and makes use of the capability to communicate about goals and tasks directly.

User requests generally reflect the larger activities that users are undertaking. A part of collaboration requires that an agent interpret the relations between simpler actions and more complex ones, so that an agent can automatically recognize the relation between the current action and more general ones. This recognition process, called *intended plan recognition* [6], can be supported algorithmically in collaborative agents so that the agent can interpret the more general purposes underlying user actions.

2.2 Collagen™-A Reusable Architecture

To support an interface agent performing as a collaborator, the research group at Mitsubishi Electric Research Laboratories has developed a Java middleware program, called Collagen™, for building COLLaborative interface AGENts to work with users on GUI applications [4, 7]. Collagen is designed with the capability to participate in collaboration and in conversation based on [1, 5] and the SharedPlan theory of collaboration [2, 3].

The spoken-language version of the Collagen architecture is shown in *Figure 2*. Collagen makes use of a *discourse state* consisting of a focus stack and a recipe tree, which is created using a combination of the discourse interpretation algorithm of [5] and plan recognition algorithms of [8, 9]. Plan recognition provides Collagen with the ability to infer how one or more actions can be used to accomplish a more general action. The *discourse interpretation* algorithm in Collagen takes as its input all user and agent utterances and interface actions, and accesses a *recipe library*. The recipes represent the actions of the domain as action types. Action types are instantiated for each activity that occurs with a particular user in a particular interaction situation. After updating the discourse state, Collagen makes two resources available to an interface agent: *the discourse state*, and an *agenda* of next possible actions computed using discourse generation from the discourse state. The Collagen middleware requires an *application adapter*, which is a sub-system that transforms the descriptions of action types and objects in the agent's internal language to program calls in the application programmer's interface (API).   The adapter also informs the discourse interpretation algorithm of any GUI events done by either the user or the agent so that these can be incorporated in the agent's understanding of the interaction.

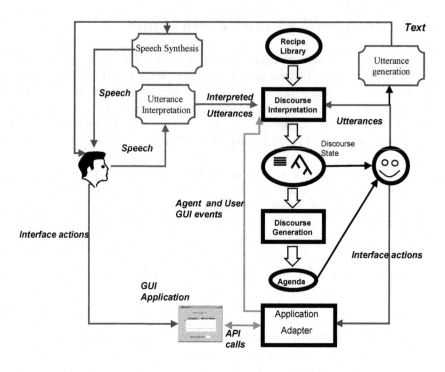

Figure 2. Collagen architecture for spoken language collaborative agents

All spoken-language agents must have a means for understanding user input and generating spoken output. In the Collagen architecture, utterance interpretation takes a spoken utterance and produces an *utterance interpretation*. Several sub-components make this possible in our spoken agents. A speech recognition engine takes user utterances and produces strings that are fed to a syntactic analyzer. The analyzer's results are semantically interpreted to form descriptions in an utterance intention language, which captures both the utterance's intentional and propositional content. Interpreted utterances are interpreted independent of context, and later processing uses the discourse state to modify the interpretation. The utterance intention language is based on an artificial discourse language [10]; it serves as the internal language for all Collagen agents. Results of semantic and intention processing are passed to the discourse interpretation module that is central in the Collagen architecture shown in *Figure 2.*

When any of the agents communicate, they make use of the Collagen facilities for *utterance generation*, which translates the internal intention language to English phrases using string template mapping. The strings are also sent to a synthesizer for speech output. Both text and spoken forms of utterances can be presented to the user. In some interfaces, the recipes in the recipe library specify special sentence forms including ones with to be spoken with emphasis.

3. FOUR SPOKEN LANGUAGE COLLABORATIVE AGENTS

Over the past several years, the Collagen team has built four spoken language collaborative interface agents as well as a number of other types of interface agents that do not involve speech [7]. Two of the spoken-language agents assisted users on business tasks, one for email (the email agent) and one for scheduling meetings with sales contacts in Notes™ databases (the scheduling agent). The other two agents, the VCR agent and the Entertainment Center agent, helped users operate time-shifted video recording systems. Each of these agents used the same underlying Collagen middleware described in Section 2 for modeling collaboration and conversation. Three of the agents used commercially available IBM speech recognition and synthesis software. The email agent used a speech recognition prototype developed at IBM's T.J. Watson Research Labs.

For each agent, a recipe library of the action types, both primitive and abstract, of the domain was created, and an adapter was programmed to access the API of the application. In addition each of the agents procedurally encoded a very small amount of specialized knowledge about activities it might perform for its domain.

3.1 The Email Agent

The email agent, shown in *Figure 3,* was the first collaborative interface agent to incorporate speech understanding and synthesis. *Figure 4* presents a conversation, which was captured from system logs, between a user and the email agent while operating the Lotus Development Corporation Esuite ™ email application. This conversation is annotated at major task boundaries for easy perusal by the reader.

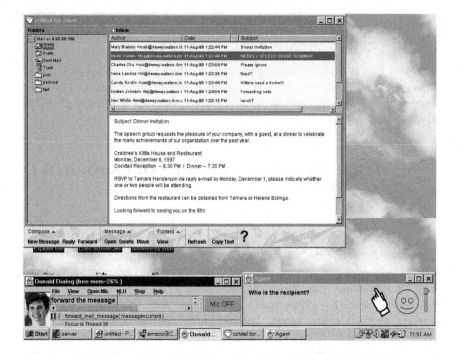

Figure 3. The email agent and Esuite email application

In this conversation, the email agent knows enough about email to undertake several tasks. It opens messages that a user selects, asks about the times for scheduling meetings and then changes the user's schedule as needed. It also knows that messages are likely to be responded to (by forwarding as well as replying) and then sent, and that email is managed by storing, printing and deleting after the message has been read.

User: "Let's work on email."
Agent: "Ok."

Choosing a message
User: Selects message from Brian Gorwin about Weekly Speech
            Group Seminar.
Agent: Opens message from Brian Gorwin about Weekly Speech
            Group Seminar.
            "Shall we use the contents of message from Brian Gorwin?

Scheduling a meeting
User: "This is about a meeting with Brian."
Agent: Setups meeting with Brian Gorwin.

"Let's schedule event tentatively at a time."
User: "Schedule the meeting at three p.m. Thursday."
Agent: Schedules event tentatively at three p.m. Thursday.
Agent: "There is a conflict of meeting with Brian Gorwin at three p.m. Thursday with meeting with Irene Landoz at three p.m. Thursday. Let's remember to re-schedule meeting with Irene Landoz at three p.m. Thursday."
User: "ok."
Agent: Finalizes meeting with Brian Gorwin at three p.m. Thursday.

Forwarding the message
"Shall we react to message from Brian Gorwin about Weekly Speech Group Seminar?
User: "Forward the message."
Agent: "Who is the recipient?"
User: "The recipient is Steve Krantz."
Agent: Presents forward template for message from Brian Gorwin about Weekly Speech Group Seminar to Steve Krantz.
"Shall we fill in message from Mary User about Fwd: Weekly Speech Group Seminar?"
User: "Ok."
Agent: Adds signature to message.
"Shall we cc message from Mary User about Fwd: Weekly Speech Group Seminar?"
User: "No."
Agent: "Ok, your turn."
User: "Send the message."
Agent: Sends the message from Mary User about Fwd: Weekly Speech Group Seminar.

Cleanup of the message
"Shall we store, print or delete this message?"
User: "Print the message."
Agent: Prints the message from Mary User about Fwd: Weekly Speech Group Seminar
Agent: "Shall we work on email?"
User: "No."

Figure 4. A conversation with the email agent

The email agent had a recipe library that described typical email actions. Of the four agents, the email agent had the largest recipe library, which included about thirty-five primitive action types (corresponding to interface action types accessible with the API), and twenty-nine non-primitive action types, with at least one, and sometimes several, recipes for non-primitives. The most general action types in the recipe library of actions are: doing email, sending email, searching email, managing email documents and reading a message. Each of these action types is described by a recipe of several steps, some steps being optional and some containing steps with partial orders. Recipes included pre and post condition tests, and they also described objects in the domain that are used in the action descriptions. For example, doing email includes the steps reading a message, responding to the message, managing the message in the inbox, and then repeating that process on additional messages.

Modelling email tasks to create a recipe library of tasks is a non-trivial undertaking because of the number of tasks in the email domain. To accomplish it, Wizard of Oz studies were conducted at Lotus in which users spoke to a human wizard as they used their email. Users could choose at any time to perform GUI operations themselves or to request that an email task (described as they wished) be performed by the wizard. User email actions were gleaned from transcripts of these sessions and described in the library.

From observing the types of conversations possible with the email agent, we concluded that the existing GUI interface precluded the agent being very helpful. In fact, the email agent actually only does very minor tasks for the user: opening and closing message windows without being asked, changing the user's schedule (when approved), and adding signatures to email messages. In large part, doing more for users would have required a very different interface so that the agent could have taken on, for example, the whole burden of constructing email messages. In designing the second agent, we decided to focus on tasks where the agent could relieve the user from as many of the time consuming details as possible.

3.2   The Scheduling Agent

The second collaborative interface agent used the Lotus product Notes[TM] and is shown in *Figure 5*. The scheduling agent was intended to help Notes users who had databases of information and who performed routine scheduling tasks involving their colleagues and clients. The agent made use of existing data in Notes databases to gather profiles, check schedules of people and rooms, and added to that data to create profiles, new meeting entries and send email messages. A sample conversation of the scheduling agent is shown in *Figure 6*.

The speech understanding sub-systems for the scheduling agent, as well as for the VCR and Entertainment Center agents, were all designed in a similar fashion. Grammars and semantic interpreters were created by the Collagen team and used with the Java Speech API as implemented by IBM, and with IBM commercially available speech recognition engines (IBM Via Voice products). Like the email agent architecture, results of semantic interpretation were passed to the discourse interpretation component of Collagen.

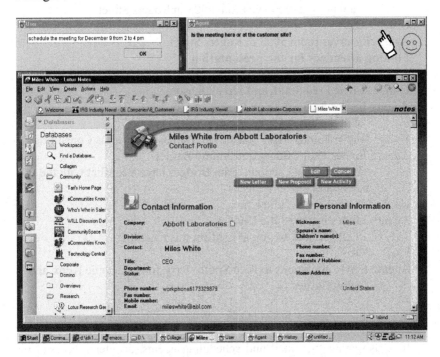

Figure 5. The scheduling agent with a Lotus Notes application

Agent: "Let's manage scheduling contacts."
Creating a profile
User: "Let's create profile for Miles White from Abbott Laboratories."
Agent: "What is the email address?"
User: "The email address is mileswhite@abl.com."
Agent: "What is the work phone?"
User: "The work phone is 617-332-9280."
Agent: Goes to profile for Abbott Laboratories.
       Creates profile for Miles White.
Scheduling a presentation
       "Do you want to schedule a presentation for Miles White?"
User: "Schedule the meeting for December 9 from 2 to 4 p.m."

Agent: Makes meeting entry for Miles White on December 9.
    "Is the meeting here or at the customer site?"
User: "The site is here."
Agent: "Which building?"
User: "The building is Rogers Street."
Agent: Locates room 5003 in Rogers Street.
    "I am going to reserve room 5003 in Rogers Street."
User: "Ok."
Agent: Reserves room 5003 in Rogers Street.

Finding attendees for the presentation
    "Who will attend the meeting?"
User: "Invite Fred Smith and Jerry Johnson."
Agent: Invites Fred Smith and Jerry Johnson.
    "Will the customer need consulting services?"
User: "Invite Pam Bridges and Jimmy Barnes from Lotus Consulting."
Agent: Invites Pam Bridges and Jimmy Barnes.
    "The following people: Pam Bridges have a conflict with the
    meeting time."
User: "Instead invite Julie Knox."
Agent: Invites instead Julie Knox.
    "I will get back to you to confirm this meeting."
User: "Ok."
Agent: Sends invitations to Fred Smith, Jerry Johnson, Julie Knox and
    Jimmy Barnes.

Figure 6. A conversation with the scheduling agent

In constructing the email and scheduling agents, adapters accessed the underlying Esuite email and Notes applications. In the case of the Notes application, the adapter did not access Notes directly but rather acted through a server, in part because Notes is not a Java application, and in part because it is a large and complex system. Details of the architectural changes for the Notes application are given in [11].

Our collaboration design goals were more successfully met for the scheduling agent than the email agent. Compared to the email agent, the scheduling contact agent undertook far more tasks for the user: it found meeting rooms in specified buildings, checked calendars for proposed participants to see if the participants were free at specified times, and sent email with preformatted invitations to proposed participants. The user was never required to oversee a GUI scheduling program. Instead, the agent simply collected the needed information and undertook appropriate scheduling tasks on its own. While only an experimental prototype, this second agent had the potential to shorten user involvement in setting up meetings with groups of participants because the user simply did not need to pay attention to the details that normally surface in GUI control of application tasks. We concluded that agents were more valuable when they offered to perform timesaving tasks for the user.

3.3   The VCR and Entertainment Center agents

The remaining two agents, the VCR agent and the Entertainment Center agent, are related because the Entertainment Center agent was a second-generation version of the VCR agent. The first of these agents was created to explore collaborative agents working with users who knew what they wanted but had never been successful in using an onscreen interface to accomplish their tasks. Since most users do not know how to program their VCRs and navigate online TV schedules, a collaborative agent was designed to take a high level simple request and gather all the details it needed itself.

The VCR agent, shown in *Figure 7*, focused on assisting a user to record programs on his VCR and also provided information about the TV schedule. A sample conversation is shown below the screen shot.

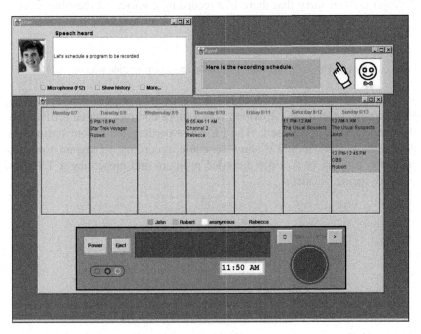

Recording a program

User: "I want to record a program."

Agent: "Here is the recording schedule."

User: "Show me the TV guide for Thursday."

Agent: [Displays TV guide for Thursday.]
       "What is the name of the program?"

User: "The program is the X-Files."

Agent: [Adds X-Files to recording schedule.]
       "Ok. What next?"

Recording a program

User: "I want to record another program."

Agent: "What is the name of the program?"

User: "It's on NBC."

Agent: "What is the starting time?"

User: "It starts at 8 p.m."

Agent: "What is the ending time?"

User: "It ends at 10 PM."

Agent: "What is the date?"

User: "Monday."

Agent: "I'm sorry that there is a recording conflict. Robert has already
       scheduled the recording of Star Trek at that time."

User: "Ok."

Figure 7. The VCR agent and application and a conversation with the agent

The Entertainment Center agent is depicted in Figure 8. It used the
Entertainment Center (EC), which was a more complex shared artifact than
the one the VCR agent used. The EC agent participated in four basic tasks:
navigating a week-long TV show schedule, recording a program from that
schedule, playing back a pre-recorded program and presenting a TV show
currently being broadcast.

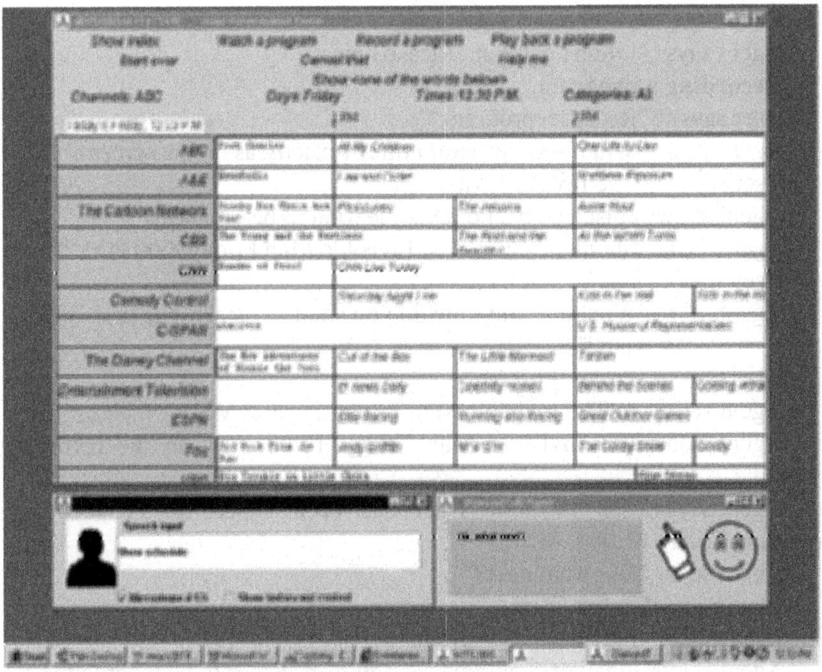

Figure 8. The Entertainment Center and Agent

While the VCR agent interpreted much more complex user utterances than the EC agent could, the simplicity of spoken language in the EC agent allowed many people to use it. A sample conversation for the EC agent is presented in *Figure 9*.

Agent says "Welcome to Diamond Talk. Try saying something shown in blue."

Navigation activities
User says   "Show schedule."
Agent says   "Ok, what next?"
User says   "Show Friday."
Agent shows schedule for Friday 12:30 A.M.
Agent says   "Ok, what next?"
User says   "Show 7 P M."
Agent shows schedule for Friday 7:00 P.M.
Agent says   "Ok, what next?"
User says "Show the W B."
Agent scrolls to the WB (channel).
Agent says   "Ok, what next?"

User says   "??? Record a program ???"
Agent says "I didn't get that. Please repeat."

Recording a program

User says   "Record a program."
Agent says "What is the program title? (exactly as on the screen)."
User says   "The Invisible Man."
Agent shows episodes of The Invisible Man to be broadcast.
Agent says "Should I record The Invisible Man Friday 8:00 P.M.?"
User says   "No."
Agent says "What day and time do you want to record The Invisible
              Man?"
User says   "Friday 11 P M."
Agent scrolls to The Invisible Man Friday 11:00 P.M.
Agent adds The Invisible Man Friday 11:00 P.M. to the recording schedule.
Agent says "The Invisible Man has been added to the recording schedule Friday 11:00 P.M."
Agent says "Ok, what next?"

Playing back a program

User says   "Play back a program."
Agent shows index of programs already recorded or to be recorded.
Agent says "What is the title of the recorded program? (exactly as on the screen)."
User says   "The Enemy Within."
Agent says "Should I play back The Enemy Within recorded Wednesday 7:30 P.M.?"
User says   "Yes."
Agent plays The Enemy Within recorded earlier.
Agent says "Ok, what next?"

Navigation activity

User says   "Show schedule."
Agent shows this week's broadcast schedule.
Agent says "Ok, what next?"
User exits.

Figure 9. A conversation with the EC agent

For navigation tasks, the EC agent simply performed the action requested by the user, while for the program tasks, the agent performed a simple form of collaboration by seeking missing information needed to do the task. When the agent was requested to do an action, it responded just as all Collagen agents can: it requested from the user the additional information that it needed, in this case, program names or channel names. Where there were several choices of times for a program of a given name, the agent also asked for clarification of times and confirmed that the user wanted to proceed. While clarification could be obtained using dialog scripting languages, the collaboration model [5] provides general agent behavior that need not be written by the system programmer. Instead, a programmer, using the collaborative interface agent framework to build an application such as this one, focuses on describing the tasks to be accomplished and leaves the conversational capabilities to the Collagen system.

3.4   A comparison of the four agents

The four dialogs between a user and a collaborative interface agent share some similarities concerning the agent's behavior and abilities. All four agents require that the user set the overall context of the interaction by providing an intention, the shared goal, to focus the interaction (for example, "Let's work on email;" "Let's create a profile for Miles White;" "I want to record a program;" or "Show schedule."). The generality of the shared goal varies significantly in these four interfaces. For the email and scheduling agents, the shared goal is very generally stated, while for the VCR and EC agents, the goals are much more specific.

The user directs the agent differently with these applications. For the email agent, the user is able to just undertake the first primitive action (selecting an email from the onscreen email inbox using the mouse) and to expect that the agent will understand how this action contributes to doing email. For the scheduling agent, the user agrees to the one overall shared activity that the agent is aware of, and then sets the direction in more detail by creating a profile for the client Miles White. The agent then begins to gather the details needed for creating the profile itself. For the VCR agent, the agent responds to the user's proposed shared goal to record a program by providing the schedule of shows already recorded and waiting for the user to determine the next action. For the EC agent, the shared goal is so directly stated that the agent can simply perform the required actions and then return the conversation to the user. All of these varieties are possible in Collagen based agents, but the variation results from the complexity of the recipe library and the way that the conversation begins.

Each of the sample dialogs differs on the use of mixed initiative in the conversation. The user initiates the email conversation, but once the agent understands the shared goal, it directs the conversation with questions about next activities and about how to accomplish a given activity. For example, given the task of forwarding the message, it asks about recipients, filling in the message and carbon copying the message to others.   In the email conversation, the user also mixes in his initiative by performing GUI actions such as selecting a message to read. In the scheduling conversation, almost all the initiative rests with the agent. By comparison, the VCR and EC conversations are much more balanced, with the user initiating each task and the agent taking initiative to ask about information that it needs.

The variation in initiative across these four examples results from experience in developing the email and scheduling agents. After building the email and scheduling agents, we concluded the user was better off having more initiative and hence more control of the interaction. To pass off initiative, the agent in the TV related applications uses the simple technique of asking "Ok, what next?" at the conclusion of each task. While this repetitive question is somewhat annoying, it clearly delineates when a task is completed and gives the user initiative and control in the conversation.

The generation capabilities of the Collagen middleware are decidedly primitive compared to that state of the art in generation research. As a result, in some conversations (especially those for email and scheduling), the agent's utterances are less natural than human ones would be. In particular, the agent does not use reduced noun phrases or pronominal forms after first mention of an object. For example, "the message from Brian Gorwin about weekly Speech Group seminar" is repeated where a reduced noun phrase would have been appropriate. Because Collagen generates language using string template matching, its techniques do not perform as well conversationally as is possible. A richer generative capability would improve the linguistic capacity of collaborative agents that must use descriptive noun phrases. This capability awaits future work in Collagen.

Collaborative interface agents understand more about conversations than just interpreting shared goals and performing tasks that contribute to those goals. They track the dialog and retain a history of it. This history, called a *segmented interaction history*, can be shown to a user (or a developer) and is a English readable "dump" of the internal data structures that are the state of the agent's understanding of the complete conversational history. *Figure 10* provides such a Collagen generated segmented interaction history for the email conversation from *Figure 4*. The conversation is segmented into units that are headed by the most general-purpose action for that segment. Segments are subdivided by more specific actions in sub-segments. The indentation illustrates to which purpose each action contributes. An early prototype of a Collagen agent for air travel planning experimented with commands to manipulate the interaction history to replay or re-use portions of the conversation [4]. In the four agents reported here, no effort has been given to these manipulations because no natural instances arose where this capability was useful. All four interface agents have segmented interaction histories that are produced as the conversation unfolds and are available at any time during the conversation.

Done working on email.
User: "Let's work on email."
Agent: "Ok."
Done reading a message from Brian Gorwin about Weekly Speech Group Seminar
Done agent selecting a message from Brian Gorwin about Weekly Speech Group Seminar
      User: Selects message from Brian Gorwin about Weekly Speech Group Seminar.
      Agent: Opens message from Brian Gorwin about Weekly Speech Group Seminar.
Done using the contents of a message from Brian Gorwin about Weekly Speech Group Seminar
      Agent: "Shall we use the contents of message from Brian Gorwin?
Done scheduling a meeting with Brian at 3 p.m. Thursday
      User: "This is about a meeting with Brian."
      Agent: Setups meeting with Brian Gorwin.
Done agent scheduling event tentatively at 3 p.m. Thursday
      Agent: "Let's schedule event tentatively at a time."
      User: "Schedule the meeting at three p.m. Thursday."
      Agent: Schedules event tentatively at three p.m. Thursday.
      Agent: "There is a conflict of meeting with Brian Gorwin at three p.m. Thursday
           with meeting with Irene Landoz at three p.m. Thursday. Let's remember to re-schedule meeting with Irene Landoz at three p.m. Thursday.
      User: "Ok."
      Agent: Finalizes meeting with Brian Gorwin at three p.m. Thursday.
Done reacting to message from Brian Gorwin about Weekly Speech Group Seminar
      Agent: "Shall we react to message from Brian Gorwin about Weekly Speech Group Seminar?"
Done forwarding the message from Brian Gorwin about Weekly Speech Group Seminar
      User: "Forward the message."
      Agent: "Who is the recipient."
      User: "The recipient is Steve Krantz."
      Agent: Presents forward template for message from Brian Gorwin about Weekly Speech Group Seminar to Steve Krantz.

Done filling in the message from Mary User about Fwd: Weekly Speech Group Seminar

Agent: "Shall we fill in message from **Mary User** about
          Fwd: Weekly Speech Group Seminar?"
User: "Ok."
Agent: Adds signature to message.
          "Shall we cc message **Mary User** about Fwd:
          Weekly Speech Group Seminar?"
User: "No."
Agent: "Ok, your turn."

Done sending, canceling or storing this message as a draft

User: "Send the message."
Agent: Sends the message from **Mary User** about Fwd:
          Weekly Speech Group Seminar.

Done storing, printing or deleting the message from Mary User about Fwd: Weekly Speech Group Seminar

Agent: "Shall we store, print or delete this message?"
User: "Print the message."
Agent: prints the message from Mary User about Fwd: Weekly
          Speech Group Seminar
Agent: "Shall we work on email?"
User: "No."

Figure 10. The segmented interaction history for an email conversation

Building these interface agents sharpened our understanding of the agent's contribution to reducing the user's burden when performing tasks. From observing the email agent and user interaction, we decided that the agent would be more effective if it could do more for the user. In building the scheduling agent, we learned that it indeed relieved the user in meeting planning of much of the painful details. For the television recording-based agents, our learning played out in a different way. Providing high level but straightforward capabilities to users meant they did not have to learn what the agent needed in advance; they could rely on the agent to request additional information that it needed. As will be discussed below, anticipating the user's needs is part of collaborative activity as well.

4. DESIGN ISSUES FOR COLLABORATIVE AGENTS

In this section we will discuss design issues in the development of the MERL EC and EC agent, the most recent agent built with Collagen. While the EC and EC agent are not intended as a commercial product, the EC agent was designed to perform with users in a realistic consumer environment. The EC and EC agent required approximately four person months of effort, from initial design to fully operational system. Because they are quite useable by an untrained user, in this section we will focus on the agent's capabilities and on lessons learned in building it. We also will discuss our visions for agent explanations to expand the tasks that the user can perform with the agent.

To understand the EC and EC agent better, first we describe the function of the entire system. Figure 8 illustrates that, in addition to the TV schedule display, windows are displayed in which the user's utterances to the agent and the agent's utterances to the user are presented. At appropriate times, windows appear for the display of the index of pre-recorded programs, for a "help me" page, for showing in simulation the currently broadcast channel, and for a list of the multiple times a program could be presented, so that the user can disambiguate at which time a program is to be recorded. With the EC, the user does not use a keyboard or a mouse, but interacts with the agent solely by speaking.

4.1 A Subset Language for the EC agent

The user cannot communicate in free form language with the EC agent. Instead the user is constrained to use what we call a *subset* language, that is, a small, artificially constructed subset of a natural language (in our examples, English) in which the user can make requests and state constraints to the agent.[2] In Figure 8, the words in bold black at the top of the TV window present the utterances that the user can say to the agent when the user is navigating the TV schedule. For every different window display that a user sees, context sensitive utterance descriptions appear. These utterances teach new users what they can say and remind experienced users in the same way. These utterances also describe the tasks that users can perform for the current application state.

---

[2] Subset languages can be contrasted with sublanguages [12] because subset languages are artificially constructed from a parent natural language and not intended to be extended by human speakers of the parent language.

The subset of English assumed in most GUI interfaces is similar to the one designed for the EC agent. However, the EC language is designed to make its membership boundaries easily inferable, so that users can reliably predict the utterances that are members of the subset language [13]. For spoken circumstances, such prediction is critical to ease of use under the constraint of real-time interaction. Because speech recognition of utterances is far from perfect, it is difficult for users to distinguish when they have mis-predicted the utterance's membership in the subset from when the recognition engine has failed (and the speech recognition subsystem provides little help in this regard). In such circumstances, users quickly become frustrated and cease interacting with speech systems. To avoid such frustrating circumstances for users, the subset language for the EC agent was designed to be simple, both syntactically and semantically. The EC agent grammar, lexicon and semantic interpretation were built at MERL; the grammar can be described by fourteen context free rules. The lexicon is medium in size, about 1100 items, of which 999 are TV show names, and twenty are TV channel names. There are no synonymous terms in the lexicon to prevent that user from either having to know which synonyms are and are not in the lexicon.

Subset languages do not offer a natural, free flowing conversational style that is typical of human speech. A subset language interaction capability was chosen due to our experience with the other three Collagen interface agents. Those agents all made use of more complex English utterances. However, in none of those systems could the user walk up and use the system without extensive speech recognition errors due to missing vocabulary or missing sentence interpretation. In those agents, users attempted to speak a wide variety of utterances that corresponded to what they wanted to do. The grammars for those agents covered some of the utterance types users would use, but none were extensive enough to cover all the user utterances. Furthermore, users could not easily be taught which utterances were allowable in the grammar because the grammar size, while not large, was large enough to preclude any type of short tutorial description. The EC agent was developed to function in conditions that were similar to the ones consumers find themselves in with new products. That is, consumers might have a user manual (which they might not look at or understand), but generally would not have someone to explain to them how to interact with the system.

The speech recognition system used with the EC agent is IBM Embedded Via Voice. It requires no training (and, in fact none is possible), and experience suggests that it understands user utterances at about 85% reliability for utterances that are correct grammatical strings for the EC agent grammar. For utterances that are not in the grammar, the EC agent does not make correct interpretations, but due to threshholding values of the recognition engine, it often says "I did not understand. Please repeat your utterance," in addition to presenting the utterance that it heard. Users are generally able to recover with this combination of information.

The Collagen team's experience with the EC agent suggests that we have progressed towards the goal of making the EC and agent usable for any speaker of English. Pilot user studies (12 subjects) show the users can use the subset created for the EC agent easily. They can perform a series of eight tasks in about eighteen minutes on average with no training on the system and no experience with speech systems. About forty more users, several non-native speakers of English, have talked with the EC agent after seeing a demo of the system. These users were all able to navigate the display, record and play back programs.

4.2 Explaining Complex Tasks to Users

Of the four basic tasks that users can undertake with the EC agent, none are as complex as the ones for email or scheduling. However, because the means to perform EC tasks were not already familiar to users, this small handful of tasks was chosen to serve the basic needs of users in conducting their TV show viewing. Simple actions, such as turning on and off the TV and changing the volume, were not included since these are already easily undertaken with existing TV remotes.

There are more complex goals that can be undertaken by the agent, and we chose to keep these from being presented to new users. Complex tasks include those for searching the TV schedule, and comparing programs. For example, the task of comparing programs requires that the agent be told the names of the programs to be compared (any number of programs can be handled this way), after which it can provide the user with descriptions of the programs. A sample such interaction is shown in *Figure 11*.

User:	Compare programs.
Agent:	What is the name of the first program?
User:	Star Trek
Agent:	In this episode of Star Trek....
Agent:	What is the name of the next program?
User:	Angel.
Agent:	In this episode of Angel....
Agent:	What is the name of the next program?
User:	No more programs.
Agent:	Want to record one of these programs?

User: Yes. Angel.

Figure 11. A sample conversation to compare programs.

It is also natural for the agent to query users at the end of this activity about the user's desire to record one of those shows because recording is a likely reason for doing comparisons. This predictive behavior allows an agent to anticipate the user's desires and to shorten the conversation. The use of plan recognition and the recipe library in Collagen makes this predictive behavior possible.

Actions such as compare programs have not yet been introduced to the EC. The delay concerns the need to better understand how users learn about more complex capabilities in agent/user interactions. Most commercial applications ignore the issue of user learning and simply provide a wide array of features to users, who must then experiment to decide which features to use. Given the dizzying array of features, users find that this trial and error process takes a long time and is quite demanding. Our design of the EC and agent proceeds in a different way. The interface displays the essential actions necessary for basic activities by presenting their invocation commands on the screen (and also providing a "help me" page where the actions are briefly described).

How are more complex actions to be presented to users? Our proposed approach makes use of two concepts: keeping track of what the user already knows how to do, and explaining new functionality to users. The Collagen middleware is already able to undertake both these activities, in part through use of a student model, and in part by using explanation recipes.

Explanations of actions that can be undertaken have been central to our research on collaborative agents. For example, in the interaction of users with email agents, users were assumed to be experienced at email use. They were able, however, to ask for the agent's understanding of how to do email. In response, the agent would step them through its understanding of the task as shown in the example dialog in *Figure 12*, taken from a system run.

User:	"What should I do?" [to read email]
Agent:	"First you read a message."
User:	"Ok."
Agent:	"Then, you might store, print or delete the message."
User:	"How do I read a message?"
Agent:	Points to where to select message.
	"First, you might select a message by clicking here."
User:	"Ok."
Agent:	Points to where to open a message.
	"Next, you open the message by clicking here."

User:	"Ok."
Agent:	"Then you might use the contents of the message. Then you might react to the message."
User:	"Ok."
Agent:	Points to where to close a message.
Agent:	"Finally , you close the message by clicking "Close" on pop-up menu here."
	Points to where to close a message.

Figure 12. Explaining how to use email

Similarly with the VCR agent, the user could ask for an explanation of how to plug in a camcorder to the VCR. In response, the agent both explained the task and did simple sensing (in simulation but consistent with the capabilities of current VCRs) to check that the user had done what the agent suggested.

These attempts reflect experienced gained with PEdogogical COllagen agents [14], better known as PACO agents. PACO agents tutor students on procedural tasks, so they can learn to do the tasks for themselves. Among PACO agent capabilities are a student model [14], which is a model to track the actions a student has been told about and those actions the student has tried performing. PACO agent facilities in Collagen are available to the more assistant-style agents used in the four spoken collaborative agents. Using PACO style tutoring, a future EC agent could employ the student model to capture the tasks that the user has used in the interface so far, before deciding it was time to introduce more complex tasks. Then the future EC agent would use an explanation recipe for comparing programs to explain that task to the user. While a student model is not used with the current EC agent, this general Collagen capability offers significant new help for users in future versions of the EC agent.

In summary, with the EC agent we have explored several aspects of user interaction with a collaborative agent. It allows the user to manage EC tasks by seeking information it needs to undertake tasks that the user specifies. To make the EC and EC agent useable by a wide range of users, we developed a highly constrained but usable spoken language, though the use of subset languages. To keep the interface tasks understandable to users, because the EC and EC agent are a new type of user interface, we provided limited but essential tasks in the interface for the user and agent to perform. To help a user learn about additional tasks that are available in the interface, we discussed how to use the tracking and explanation capabilities of Collagen for additional user tasks.

5.   RELATED WORK

The field of conversational speech interfaces has grown enormously in the past few years (see [15]). Rather than a comprehensive treatment of all such works, a few relevant systems will be reviewed here. The most sophisticated conversational speech interface developed to date is the VERBMOBIL system [16]. This speech-to-speech conversational system translated each user's input to a conversation in the languages of German, Japanese and English. The discussion domain was travel matters, hotel reservations and ticketing. While VERBMOBIL did not use an agent that must contribute to a conversation, its overall dialog capabilities were quite rich. The dialog management subcomponent generated dialog summaries, and it classified all utterances according to their utterance type before proceeding to speech translation.

Glass and Weinstein [17] report on SpeechBuilder, a facility for quickly developing spoken dialog systems. The architecture relied on the Galaxy Hub architecture [18] and the types of utterances available were restricted to those that are semantically related to case frame filling. SpeechBuilder used the dialog manager of the Galaxy architecture, which was limited to a dialog state variable rather than the more general models used in VERBMOBIL, Collagen, Artimis [19] or Allen's TRIPS and TRAINS systems.

Allen's recent TRIPS system [20], a follow-on to the TRAINS system, focused on producing and interpreting spoken language in an incremental fashion. This system is aiming to interpret utterances that were partially complete, contained pauses, or were grounded by acknowledgements such as "mm-mm." Like the TRAINS system, TRIPS had a rich model of dialog, separated domain and dialog reasoning and modelled turn taking explicitly.

6.   A RECAP OF LESSONS LEARNED

Collaboration is essential to spoken language conversational systems. Users converse with computer applications in order to accomplish tasks with those applications. Without collaboration, the user is forced to manage the entire task himself, and must be very literal in what he asks the computer to do for him. With collaboration, the user can delegate parts of the tasks for the agent to perform, and respond to agent requests for information it needs to accomplish the task on the user's behalf.

In this article, we have reported on our experience with four collaborative interface agents for GUI applications. All these agents make use of their knowledge of the conversational structure, the intentions of the user and agent and the relations between the two to perform tasks in service of the shared goals. Our agents are most effective in collaboration when the application provides significant sub-tasks that the agent can undertake on behalf of the user. Even in those cases where the sub-tasks are simple, the ability of the agent to decide itself what information it needs, reduces the user burden in managing the details of the actions that contribute to the shared goals.

Human collaborations are far richer than those that can be undertaken with computer agents, in part because people know and can do more than our computer systems. Equally important, human collaborations involve richer conversations than users can yet have with their collaborative agents due to the limitations of speech technology. Our experience with collaborative interface agents indicates that for GUI applications, spoken conversations are effective and can be available to many users by employing a subset language of a natural language.

REFERENCES

[1] B. J. Grosz and C. L. Sidner, "Attention, intentions, and the structure of discourse," *Computational Linguistics*, vol. 12, pp. 175-204, 1986.

[2] B. Grosz and C. L. Sidner, "Plans for discourse," in *Intentions and Plans in Communication and Discourse*, P. Cohen, J. Morgan, and M. Pollack, Eds. Cambridge, MA, USA: MIT Press, 1990.

[3] B. Grosz and S. Kraus, "Collaborative plans for complex group action," *Artificial Intelligence*, vol. 86, pp. 269-357, 1996.

[4] C. Rich and C. L. Sidner, "COLLAGEN: A collaboration manager for software interface agents," *User modeling and user adapted interaction*, vol. 8, pp. 315-350, 1998.

[5] K. E. Lochbaum, "A Collaborative Planning Model of Intentional Structure," *Computational Linguistics*, vol. 24, pp. 525-572, 1998.

[6] P. Cohen, R. Perrault, and J. Allen, "Beyond Question Answering," in *Strategies for Natural Language Processing*, W. Lehnert and M. Ringle, Eds. Hillsdale, NJ, USA: Lawrence Erlbaum Associates, 1982, pp. 245-274.

[7] C. Rich, C. L. Sidner, and N. B. Lesh, "COLLAGEN: Applying Collaborative Discourse Theory to Human-Computer Interaction," in *AI Magazine, Special Issue on Intelligent User Interfaces*, vol. 22, 2001, pp. 15-25.

[8] N. B. Lesh, C. Rich, and C. L. Sidner, "Collaborating with focused and unfocused users," presented at Proceedings of the 8th International Conference on User-Modeling, 2001.

[9] N. B. Lesh, C. Rich, and C. L. Sidner, "Using Plan Recognition in Human-Computer Interaction," presented at Proceedings of the 7th International Conference on User Modeling, 1999.

[10] C. L. Sidner, "An artificial discourse language for collaborative negotiation," presented at Proceedings of the Twelfth National Conference on Artificial Intelligence, 1994.

[11] C. L. Sidner, C. Boettner, and C. Rich, "Building spoken language collaborative interface agents," in *Lotus Technical Report TR2001-01*: Lotus Development Corporation, 2001.

[12] R. Kittredge, "Variation and Homogeneity of Sublanguages," in *Sublanguage: Studies of language in restricted semantic domains*, R. Kittredge and J. Lehrberger, Eds. Berlin and New York: de Gruyter, 1982, pp. 107-137.

[13] C. L. Sidner and C. Forlines, "Subset language for conversing with collaborative interface agents," presented at Proceedings of the 2002 International Conference on Spoken Language Processing, 2002.

[14] J. Rickel, N. B. Lesh, C. Rich, C. L. Sidner, and A. Gertner, "Collaborative discourse theory as a foundation for tutorial dialogue," presented at Proceedings of the Sixth International Conference on Intelligent Tutoring Systems, 2002.

[15] C. L. Sidner, *ANLP/NAACL 2000 Workshop on Conversational Systems,* Association for Computational Linguistics, 2000.

[16] W. Wahlster, *Verbmobil: Foundations of Speech-To-Speech Translation,* Springer-Verlag, 2000.

[17] J. Glass and E. Weinstein, "SpeechBuilder. facilitating spoken dialog system development," presented at Proceedings of Eurospeech 2001, Alborg, Denmark, 2001.

[18] S. Seneff, R. Lau, and J. Polifroni, "Organization, communication, and control in the Galaxy-II Conversational System," presented at Proceedings of Eurospeech 1999, Budapest, 1999.

[19] M. D. Sadek, P. Bretier, and F. Panaget, "ARTIMIS: Natural dialogue meets rational agency," presented at Proceedings of IJCAI-97, Nagoya, Japan, 1997.

[20] J. Allen, G. Ferguson, and A. Stent, "An architecture for more realistic conversational systems," presented at Proceedings of the 2001 Conference on Intelligent User Interfaces, New York, 2001.

INDEX

Printed in the United States
By Bookmasters